PUBLIC RELATIONS

&

the SUSTAINABLE DEVELOPMENT GOALS

Case Studies in Practice

Marking 25 years of the TU Dublin M.A. in Public Relations

·OAK·TREE·PRESS·

Edited by:

Kevin Hora
Cliodhna Pierce
Isaac Antwi-Boasiako

corporate group

Published by Oak Tree Press, Cork T12 XY2N, Ireland.
www.oaktreepress.com / www.SuccessStore.com

© 2024 Kevin Hora, Cliodhna Pierce & Isaac Antwi-Boasiako

Cover design: Kieran O'Connor Design.

A catalogue record for this book is available from the British Library.
ISBN 978-1-78119-628-1 Paperback
ISBN 978-1-78119-629-1 PDF
ISBN 978-1-78119-630-4 ePub
ISBN 978-1-78119-631-1 Kindle

Contents

Introduction

Kevin Hora, Cliodhna Pierce and Isaac-Antwi-Boasiako

The first graduates from the Dublin Institute of Technology's (DIT) M.A. in Public Relations in 1999 were a combination of full-time students and 'converts' – graduates who had completed DIT's Postgraduate Diploma in Public Relations in the preceding five years. They were also graduates of the first programme awarded at Master's level by DIT under its own degree conferring powers, a circumstance that owed much to the prescience of the programme founder, Dr. Francis Xavier Carty, FPRII. Over the subsequent 25 years, hundreds of the programme's graduates have become a distinctive cohort in the Irish public relations landscape, rising to senior executive ranks in consultancy, corporate and civic society, as founders of their own consultancies and award-winning practitioners, or bringing their skills as strategic communications practitioners to other sectors and industries, including academia where their research and publications explore new boundaries in communications. Others have travelled, bringing their qualification to the core of the European Union in Brussels, to the UK, North America and Australia. At the same time, international graduates have returned to their homelands in Asia, Africa, South America and throughout Europe.

At the heart of the programme's continued success has been dedication to blending theory and practice to produce public relations practitioners equipped to think critically about communications and their responsibilities as communicators. This commitment to excellence in education and ethical standards has seen the programme become the only Irish public relations course recognised by the Public Relations Institute of Ireland, the Public Relations Society of America and the Chartered Institute of Public Relations in the UK – the latter two accreditations owing much to the vision of F.X. Carty's successor as Programme Chair, Dr. John Gallagher, FPRII.

Over a quarter of a century, it has been the case that *plus ça change, plus c'est la même chose*: DIT has become Technological University Dublin, Ireland's first and largest technological university; the programme has moved to a purpose-built campus in Grangegorman where students have access to media and broadcast facilities that outstrip industry standards; Dr. Kevin Hora MPRII, himself a convert from 1999, took up the role of programme chair in succession to John Gallagher, and, in turn, was succeeded by the present incumbent, Dr. Cliodhna Pierce. In industry, new language and terminology has evolved as the role of strategic communications has become more nuanced, and practitioners are more aware of their societal responsibilities. Where once public relations students learned that the best sponsorship was truly altruistic, then later students about the corporate conscience, now sustainability is embedded in their studies, in a theory and practice informed journey that has embraced corporate social responsibility (CSR) and environmental, social and governance (ESG) norms. The curriculum has evolved from examining the role of women in the industry through a male lens, to appreciating the multifaceted complexities, values and contributions of gender, ethnicity and neurodiversity, amongst others, to realising a programme reflective of society. Notwithstanding these conceptual evolutions, the standard of students on the programme has not diminished, as evidenced in this collection of case studies focusing on the role of strategic communications in helping organisations to meet the United Nation's Sustainable Development Goals (SDGs).

Of the myriad themes that could have been explored, why choose sustainability? Indeed, why choose a theme at all? The 1995 cohort of the MA's precursor, the Postgraduate Diploma in Public Relations, were, under F.X. Carty, responsible for the near-legendary compendium of Irish public relations case studies *From John Paul to Saint Jack*, a book that transcended industries, sectors and specialisations, and, even today, has case studies in which a keen reader will see proto-sustainability. In his introduction, Carty wrote that public relations is the organisation's conscience, which guides it towards the public good. "They have", he wrote, "a moral duty to engage in it" (Carty, 1995). A similar moral imperative underpins TU Dublin, which has the SDGs at the core of its strategic purpose, encapsulated as people, planet and partnership. The School of Media, where the M.A. in Public Relations resides, is explicit in its mission "to link the cultural, technological and societal, to encourage debate, foster lifelong learning, produce imaginative, practical innovations and solutions, and give voice to the matters that impact on society".

Sustainability, therefore, is intrinsic to the programme's core content and underlying pedagogical principles, which have evolved in tandem with industry practice and academic research. There is, however, a *lacuna* in the academic literature regarding the practice of public relations for sustainability purposes, where a sizeable cohort of authors are concerned with how public relations can deliver sustainability goals for an organisation's benefit. While organisations should aspire to be sustainable, clearly, this perspective is the opposite of acting in enlightened self-interest: "recognising that when your organisation acts responsibly towards society it also benefits" (Hora, 2014). Thus, Rivero & Theodore: "The role of the corporation in the social area of sustainability is based on socially responsible investtments [*sic*].... Public relations is directed toward stakeholder groups and investment / financial centres" (Rivero & Theodore, 2014). Ditlev-Simonsen (2022) notes that a study of the S&P 500 discovered that sustainability was linked to profit by 69% of firms, to people by 34% and the planet by just 14%. She also suggests that when firms began generating social responsibility reports as part of, or supplementary to, annual financial reports, this work was farmed out to public relations firms.

Hers is an implicit criticism that public relations practitioners were hired for their ability to frame messages in ways that advantaged clients or altered discourses in their favour. Roper notes the prevalence of public relations providing a quick fix to an issue without addressing the substantive matter (Roper, 2013). Motion & Leitch capture the hired gun *leitmotif* succinctly, though their focus is on interrogating the Foucauldian concept of truth as a means of problematising practice, and they do not advocate either of the following practices:

> A public relations practitioner may attempt to change environmental discourse boundaries by introducing an economic discourse of growth and job security, position opponents as 'greenie' radicals or ecoterrorists, focus on the language of business, finance, and job security, and attempt to influence unions. Or, conversely, public relations practitioners may attempt to overturn such efforts by reasserting the economic value of sustainability, position opponents as irresponsible corporations, and focus on climate change (Motion & Leitch, 2009).

Holmström leans into more recognisably sustainable territory with her examination of reflexive and reflective organisations: while initially risky for organisations as it opens them up to scrutiny about their core mission, the latter produces best practices "which are adaptable to basic existing structures in the form of, for instance, certification, verification, sustainability accounts, and business guidelines for social responsibility" (Holmström, 2009). The process is still, however, predicated from the organisation's position.

Robert L. Heath has long advocated that public relations "should focus on adding value to society rather than solely to clients" (Roper, 2013). Genç follows this line of reasoning with a perceptive approach that splits sustainability communication into three distinct categories: about, of and for. With respect to the first, it is an informative and discursive exchange process with internal and external audiences; in the second, power in the communications relationship rests with the sender, who identifies a strategic objective that they wish the audience should know; the only feedback sought is confirmation of acquiescence or behavioural change by the target public. The third takes as its premise that communication is not merely informative of corporate standpoints or raising awareness of sometimes questionable claims but co-creates genuine societal transformation through the prism of sustainable development goals (Genç, 2017). This perspective informs the 12 case studies in this collection. Public relations is not considered here as a tool for corporate self-aggrandisement but as a vital, inseparable element of the sustainability goals themselves. When responses to sustainability issues range from co-operation to hostility, strategic communications that identifies audiences and their issues to engage in effective, dialogic communication with them is paramount.

The 12 case studies in this book were each selected, researched and written by a member of the 25th student cohort. Each was chosen according to the student's sectoral, personal, or other interest to use the case to illustrate how effective strategic communications can help bring to fruition a campaign that addresses a sustainable development goal. The focus, therefore, is on the communications that inform and motivate actions and behaviours rather than the intrinsic nature of the goals themselves. With each addressing a particular goal, there are case studies from Ireland and abroad, reflecting the diversity of the cohort. While the cases are written to make them accessible to readers approaching public relations for the first time or to time-constrained practitioners, the more advanced public relations student will see where they may be applied to illustrate advanced theoretical concepts. A short series of questions at the end of each case study will be helpful for educators as a teaching tool for further exploration and reflection, while three intermezzo chapters by the book's editors offer additional critical interpretations to stimulate deeper considerations.

Opening the first trio of case studies, Nimra Ahmed takes as her focal point SDG 1 – No Poverty, with an examination of the Children's Rights Alliance's *End Child Poverty Week* campaign. Founded in 1995, the organisation's 2023 campaign focused on child poverty in multiple aspects: educational inequality, child welfare and alternative care, national and local actions and plans, income, and early years. Its focus was to provide evidence and solutions to break the children's and young people's cycle of poverty and bring pressure to bear on the Irish government to prioritise child welfare. Avice Meya continues with an Irish sustainability movement that has created global momentum to address SDG 2 – Zero Hunger. The Grow It Yourself (GIY) movement was founded by Michael Kelly in 2008 to address global challenges in the broken food system. Through inclusive and accessible partnerships and education about food growing programmes to communities and schools, GIY emphasises the importance of localised, community-driven initiatives to reimagine and revitalise sustainable food systems as central to food security, nutrition, and sustainable agriculture. Eve Wright's case study concerns SDG 3 – Good Health & Well-being, with a focus on Target 3.5, the prevention and treatment of the harmful use of alcohol. A challenge to public health in Ireland, excessive alcohol consumption costs the State almost €2 billion annually in health-related costs, and contributes to over 1,500 deaths. Alcohol Action Ireland's campaign to implement minimum unit pricing 10 years after it was first proposed, in the face of concerted drinks industry opposition, demonstrates the long vision necessary for sustainability progress.

Isaac Antwi-Boasiako's intermezzo chapter takes a discursive dimension of public relations and the SDG discourse by exploring how PR paradigms can serve as a communication framework for promoting and advancing the sustainable development goals' agenda to the global community. It espouses the relevance of public relations paradigms such as Excellence and its models, relationship management, and rhetoric to the SDGs. The chapter also introduces the Ubuntu concept as a potential PR paradigm. A philosophical concept with origins across Africa, Ubuntu can be considered in developing strategic communication frameworks to promote and create awareness of the SDGs. Though not classified officially or traditionally as a PR paradigm in the strategic communications discourse, the principles of Ubuntu philosophy, such as interconnectedness, cooperation, collective well-being, and interdependence of individuals within a community, can be incorporated into PR practice in general, and in the context of designing sustainable development communication activities, in particular. The chapter argues that PR paradigms provide a strategic platform for building practical and achievable communication campaigns by stakeholders promoting the SDGs. This aligns with a conviction that sustainable development communication campaigns need to be built on the theoretical and practical principles enshrined in the explored PR paradigms, such as engagement, persuasion, dialogue, interdependence and mutual relationships, depending on the goal of the campaign and the targeted audiences, both national and international. By leveraging these PR paradigms with SDGs, advocates, both state and non-state actors, can enhance their communication strategies. This can be achieved through building and maintaining mutually beneficial relationships and partnerships with strategically targeted audiences to attain global sustainable goals on a large scale.

Molly Reilly continues the case studies with a focus on SDG 5 – Gender Equality, particularly Target 5.5, relating to women's participation and decisionmaking role in political, economic and public life, with her study of WorkEqual in Ireland. This organisation highlighted the gender pay gap and advocated for improved caring responsibilities to be properly recognised by policymakers and employers. These included a better childcare system that would enable parents to fully participate in the workforce, and accessible early years care and education for children. In the first case study to take an international perspective, Dylan Mahon looks at the International Reference Centre on Community Water Supply and the UN's Water, Sanitation & Hygiene (WASH) initiative under SDG 6 – Clean Water & Sanitation. His work details a strategic collaboration between the IRC and the Ghanaian government to achieve progress in the WASH initiative that addressed districts, ministries, NGOs and government agencies in a campaign that blended communications and public education. Sean Ivory returns to Ireland with SDG 7 – Affordable & Clean Energy to examine how the Tyndall Institute, a research institute of University College Cork, worked with the Sustainable Energy Authority of Ireland to further Tyndall's mission towards decarbonisation and energy efficiency. Against the background of the Irish government's 2030 decarbonisation requirements, one of the key physical challenges for the campaign was upgrading Tyndall's Kiln building, originally constructed in 1903, and contributing through action to the dialogue promoting investment in sustainable energy.

Cliodhna Pierce's intermezzo chapter looks at public relations literature in terms of the publics and various stakeholders with whom organisations interact. Due to its journalistic roots, PR initially approached publics as largely passive audiences – homogenous groups segmented by demographics, geographics, or psychographics to facilitate targeted messaging. A recent shift, however, emphasises the importance of building genuine relationships with stakeholders. Over the past two decades, PR scholarship has expanded significantly, incorporating influences from digital media, network theory, political economy, cultural studies, and institutional theory. Critical theory perspectives such as feminism and critical race theory have also gained prominence, offering previously marginalised analyses of power dynamics within PR (L'Etang, 2016).

For understanding in the field of communication, concepts like problem recognition, constraint recognition, and a person's level of situational involvement are key for tailoring effective communication strategies to make them highly relevant communication tools. Proactive PR practitioners apply these concepts to anticipate how publics will respond to their messages. Core theories continue to evolve, providing increasingly sophisticated tools for navigating complex stakeholder environments. These tools help practitioners understand the active role of publics in shaping discourse, the importance of two-way dialogue, and the power dynamics at play in diverse social arenas.

Contemporary PR theory underscores the fluidity of publics as they actively try to shape issues and influence organisational decisions. As stated by Jones (2001):

> The mistakes of contemporary public relations theory [lie] in defining publics as being either latent or active... and then categorising them strategically according to how they might affect the organisation... it offers no insight into the internal dynamics of publics and the ways in which they construct the issue at hand.

Crucially, even when an organisation interacts with a specific public segment, that group is embedded within a broader discourse network that significantly shapes its positions on relevant issues. PR professionals must recognise these dynamics to develop impactful communication strategies that promote both organisational success and positive social change. Therefore, sustainable and effective communication necessitates a deep understanding of current public perceptions of the SDGs. This chapter examines four key theoretical perspectives, situational theory, systems theory, Chay-Nemeth's theory, and linkage theory, and analyses how they can be leveraged to enhance public buy-in for the SDGs.

Having worked for the organisation, Gabriela Doleckova used her insight to discover more about Caritas Czech Republic's *Meaningful Gift* campaign, which addresses SDG 8 – Decent Work & Economic Growth. Among the campaign's broad aims is the ambition of enhancing the economic self-sufficiency of individuals in developing nations through education and vocational training. Her study explores how a human-centric approach to the campaign used elements that ranged from alignment with SDG 8 to strategic communications tactics. Hate crime and its importance within SDG 10 – Reduced Inequalities is the concern of Tess Thornton's work. The Coalition Against Hate Crime Ireland (CAHCI) *Hate Crime Hurts Us All* campaign, with support from We The People, a specialised communications agency, addressed the absence of dedicated hate crime legislation in Ireland. The campaign tackled rising hate-related incidents, using a strategy that featured real individuals and strategic influencer engagement to raise awareness and advocate for government legislation on hate crime for a more inclusive, equitable society. Although the hotel sector has long been accused of greenwashing, David Little's study of The Salthouse Hotel in Northern Ireland's County Antrim shows how SDG 11 – Sustainable Cities & Communities can be achieved through sustainable business practices. With its own onsite wind turbine and solar panels, the hotel, which has won awards for its sustainability efforts, is energy self-sufficient, while its ethos centres on promoting responsible eco-tourism that is attuned to its Atlantic Ocean setting.

The final intermezzo chapter by Kevin Hora looks at the tactics and activities employed in the various campaigns through pragmatic and theoretical lenses. He probes to distinguish the difference between methods used because they are considered good practice, and thus offer an off-the-shelf approach to strategic communication campaigns, and methods that demonstrate higher levels of strategic creativity. His chapter contends that, while there is a place for tactics that are as familiar to practitioners as they are to audiences, the difficulties of communications for sustainability (where like-minded organisations are clamouring to be heard individually; the gamut of sustainability concerns has exponentially increased; and hostility from vested interests is orchestrated using similar communications tactics) mean that organisations have to be strategically creative. Creativity, he notes, is not simply about generating clever ideas: it is the end output in a strategic process that begins with empathy for the issue and publics, apprises the context, and rearranges the perspective to produce engaging actions and outcomes. From this, he progresses to examine storytelling as a creative process. Storytelling has become a cliché in strategic communications, reductively a linear narrative process. The craft of storytelling is subservient to creating a narrative that the organisation wants to tell, not one the audience wants to hear. He introduces Propp's morphology of the folk tale as a means of structuring compelling stories centred around themes, characters, action and plot. Recognising that compelling storytelling is rooted in rhetoric, he finishes the chapter by demonstrating how Burkean dramatism theory and the dramatistic pentad may be used as part of the creative process for sustainability communications.

Martha O'Brien's study highlights an organisation that discovered that tried and tested methods in creating dialogues in other arenas of concern were less effective when deployed for SDG 13 – Climate Action. Friends of the Earth's *Cuppa for Climate* campaign used the popular coffee-morning activity to generate conversations about climate awareness in a friendly, supportive environment, removed from climate denial and hostility. However, as the case study shows, this was a slightly artificial environment that yielded modest results, and the real learning came from the organisation's ability to amend its approach. Jade Marron takes SDG 15 – Life on Land, exemplified by Leave No Trace Ireland's annual campaign *Love This Place*, as her domain of inquiry. The campaign started in the early months of Covid-19 in Ireland, when people isolating from the virus took to the outdoors to socialise within permitted governmental rules. For many, this experience of nature was novel and, as they did not appreciate the norms and etiquette of appreciating the environment, a spike in littering and environmental issues ensued. Building on raising awareness about enjoying the outdoors responsibly, the campaign has continuously evolved new messages each year. The final case study by Sarah-Kate Spratt deals with human trafficking. The *Anyone* campaign, a collaborative effort between the Department of Justice and the UN Migration Office in Ireland, aligns with SDG 16 – Peace, Justice & Strong Institutions. Launched in 2021, *Anyone* aims to educate the public about human trafficking using a variety of communications tactics, including the powerful short film, *Anyone: Deceived*, a dedicated website with informational videos, case studies, resources, and social media.

The case studies and intermezzo chapters in this book would not have been possible without the support and collaboration of colleagues. The editors gratefully acknowledge a bursary from the Strategic Alignment of Teaching & Learning Enhancement (SATLE) Fund dispensed through the Faculty of Arts and Humanities that facilitated research space and mentoring. Seán Finnan, a doctoral researcher in the School of Media, provided invaluable research and writing direction to the students. Dr. Caroline Ann O'Sullivan, Head of the School of Media, was supportive from the outset. Most credit, however, goes, to the students of the 25th cohort who embraced the challenge of writing for publication, and leave for future cohorts – and learners, academics and practitioner everywhere – this collection.

References

Carty, F.X. (1995). *From John Paul to Saint Jack*. Dublin: Able Press.

Ditlev-Simonsen, C.D. (2022). *A Guide to Sustainable Corporate Responsibility: From Theory to Action*. London: Palgrave Macmillan.

Genç, R. (2017). The importance of communication in sustainability and sustainable strategies. *Procedia Manufacturing*, pp.511-516.

Holmström, S. (2009). On Luhmann: Contingency, Risk, Trust, & Reflection. In: Ø. Ihlen, B. van Ruler & M. Fredriksson (eds.). *Public Relations & Social Theory: Key Figures & Concepts*. Abingdon, Oxon: Routledge.

Hora, K. (2014). *Quick Win Public Relations: Answers to Your Top 100 Public Relations Questions*. Cork: Oak Tree Press.

Jones, R. (2001). Challenges to the notion of publics in public relations: Implications of the risk society for the discipline. *Public Relations Review*, 28(1), pp.49-62.

L'Etang, J. (2016). Public relations, activism and social movements: Critical perspectives. *Public Relations Inquiry*, 5(3), pp.207-211.

Motion, J. & Leitch, S. (2009). On Foucault: A Toolbox for *Public Relations. In: Ø. Ihlen, B. van Ruler & M. Fredriksson, (eds.). Public Relations & Social Theory: Key Figures & Concepts*. Abingdon, Oxon: Routledge.

Rivero, O. & Theodore, J. (2014). The importance of public relations in corporate sustainability. *Global Journal of Management & Business Research*, 14(4), pp. 1-23.

Roper, J. (2013). Sustainability as a Global Challenge. In: R.L. Heath (ed.). *Encyclopaedia of Public Relations*. Thousand Oaks, CA: Sage.

I. SDG 1 – No Poverty

The Children's Rights Alliance's *End Child Poverty Week* Campaign

Nimra Ahmed

Abstract

This case study explores one of the Children's Rights Alliance's (CRA) campaigns designed to highlight the impact of child poverty and provide plausible solutions to the Irish government. Founded in 1995, the CRA champions the rights of vulnerable children in Ireland, aiming to ensure their voices are heard, needs met, and rights protected through laws and services. This mission is reflected in new government commitments addressing childhood obesity, food poverty, child poverty, and support for victims within the National Policy Framework for Children & Young People. The CRA's 2023 *End Child Poverty Week* campaign targeted issues like educational inequality and child welfare, driving change with evidence and innovative solutions. This effort aligns with the UN's Sustainable Development Goal 1 to halve global poverty by 2030.

Introduction

Food poverty is defined as the lack of capacity to have an adequate, nutritious diet because of issues of affordability or accessibility. Over the past decade, food poverty has become a pressing social policy in Ireland. The Children's Rights Alliance's *End Child Poverty Week* campaign has emerged as a dynamic force that empowers its members to pinpoint the challenges children and young people face and forge solutions that transform lives for the better. They scrutinise existing laws through meticulous research and insightful analysis, expose gaps in services and policies, and ignite campaigns that educate, inform, and propose tangible solutions to policymakers. This advocacy ensures children's issues are front and centre, aligning perfectly with SDG 1's ambitious aim to "reduce poverty by half of the proportion of men, women and children living in poverty in all its dimensions".

Discussing child food poverty casts a harsh reality where families are forced to make difficult choices, sacrificing the quantity and quality of their children's meals to survive. In Ireland, 17.94% of children aged 15 years or below lived with moderate or severe food insecurity. More strikingly, one in five children affected by food poverty go to bed or school hungry simply because there is no food at home.

Identifying SDGs & Targets

SDG 1 has ambitious aims: to ensure that everyone, especially the impoverished and most vulnerable, are prosperous, and they have social protection through essential supports and services, from social welfare to child payment and access to health care. Increasingly, in light of emerging global conflicts, vital support has expanded for people fleeing war, climate-related disasters and other economic, social and environmental shocks. Ireland's vision, to be one of world's best small countries in which to grow up and raise a family, is hugely ambitious. To make this aspirational goal a reality, the Irish Government must focus on and create pro-impoverishment and gender-sensitive policy frameworks to mobilise resources to support investment in alleviating poverty.

According to the most recent *Survey of Income & Living Conditions* (SILC), the number of children living in poverty or deprivation rose to 236,910. The number of children living in consistent poverty rose from 5.2% to 7.5%, almost 90,000 children. The poverty target set by the Irish government aims to reduce the national consistent poverty rate to 2% or less by 2025. In conjunction with this target, the CRA, as part of its ongoing campaign, aims to establish a Child Poverty Members Steering Group to include key influential leaders from various sectors to guide and direct its work dedicated to alleviating child poverty. Over three years, it aims to run a yearly *End Child Poverty Week* campaign that coincides with the annual Budget Day. CRA will recommend and participate in projects to highlight and address inequalities, published in an annual *Child Poverty Monitor* report. The findings in the report will identify gaps where children and young people continue to experience poverty and will be instrumental in setting out the organisation's National Policy Framework for children and young people.

Background

Established in 1995, the Children's Rights Alliance has 150 members who work together to ensure children's and young people's rights in Ireland are respected and protected in laws, policies, and services. Through its work, the organisation sets out key recommendations which shape and direct government policies centred around children and young people. These policy changes seek to alleviate pressing issues that impact children's and young people's lives. One critical early success, for example, was its role in the 2002 campaign that established Ireland's first Office of the Ombudsman for Children & Young People, a landmark achievement. A further victory for the organisation occurred in 2012 when it campaigned and won the referendum to strengthen children's constitutional rights.

Now called the Ombudsman for Children's Office (OCO), in a recent report it recorded that 16,804 children live in hotels and emergency accommodations. As a result, the CRA conducted a nine-month *No Child 2020* campaign, which listed five fundamental goals: no child should be hungry, homeless, without timely, affordable healthcare; blocked from having an education, or excluded from culture and sport. The campaign was central to obtaining government commitments on childhood obesity, food poverty, child poverty, and support for child victims in the National Policy Framework for Children & Young People.

In 2022, findings from SILC indicated that the at-risk of poverty rate increased from 11.6% in 2021 to 13.1%. Considering the stark finding in the 2022 report, it became more pressing that the poverty facing vulnerable children be addressed, and the CRA hosted a campaign, *End Child Poverty Week 2023*, that brought together 19 members, stakeholders, experts and state officials to focus on the impact of child poverty and provide plausible solutions to the Government. The campaign focused on the importance of early childhood interventions, particularly those aimed at breaking the cycle of poverty in a child's formative years. This work highlighted the need for improved public services like education and housing, child welfare and alternative care, national and local actions / plans, income, and targeted support to reach Ireland's most vulnerable children.

Coinciding with its annual flagship event, the CRA also publishes the yearly *Child Poverty Monitor*, launched in 2022, to analyse, report, and document child poverty in Ireland. This report tracks the government's progress, highlights solutions, and spotlights critical areas of concern across issues like food poverty and income adequacy. In conjunction with the annual *Monitor*, it issues a 'report card' that examines how the government delivers on its commitments to children.

Tactics & Activities

The 2030 Agenda acknowledges that eradicating poverty in all its forms and dimensions, including extreme poverty, is the greatest global challenge and an indispensable requirement for sustainable development. The CRA is a well-established organisation with a solid online presence of over 20,000 followers on X (formerly Twitter), 10,000 on Facebook, and an active YouTube channel where it showcases its *End Child Poverty Week* campaign. The 2023 campaign had several talks and seminars explicitly focusing on early years to break the cycle of poverty early in a child's life, the need for improved public services, housing and education, and the need for targeted support to reach children most in need. The campaign aims to keep child poverty at the top of the political agenda through new initiatives: the launch of a new research series tracking the government's performance on reducing child poverty – the *Child Poverty Monitor* – and the co-ordination of *End Child Poverty Week* to strengthen budget demands to deliver real change for children. The CRA will monitor and document the progress of the no-poverty campaigns over the years.

In 2022, the CRA addressed food poverty by addressing 'holiday hunger' families. Because school was shut for the summer, food provision was given to 660 children in 242 families. Further funds were also collected for Christmas. Under sustained advocacy from the CRA, in December 2022, the Taoiseach announced that a new Child Poverty & Well-being Unit would be formed.

In 2023, the CRA had a *1,2,3 Online Safety campaign* and campaigned for crucial amendments to the *Online Safety & Media Regulation* (OSMR) *Bill,* including establishing a devoted Online Safety Commissioner and individual issues mechanism to protect children and young people's rights online. In conjunction with the campaign, the CRA held a total of 12 meetings for members with a range of agencies, including UNICEF Ireland, Tusla, the National Coordinating Response Forum, Euro Child, the UNHCR Ireland, the Department of Education, and the Department of Children, Equality, Disability, Integration, & Youth. The CRA's *Know Your Rights Information Guide* for refugees was updated. Presenting a united front, the CRA provided recommendations to the government to help formulate policies that can impact the lives of impoverished children – a core tenet of SDG 1.

The CRA, in its communications strategy, compiles statistics to advocate directly or indirectly to various agencies and people involved in children's poverty. Its *End Poverty Week* seminars, which run in tandem with their published reports, focus on children's poverty annually and highlight areas where the government needs to step in, push for more allowances, work harder to collect funds, and change legislation if required. The seminars were recorded and published on the CRA's YouTube channel and Facebook, along with calls to donate.

Results & Outcomes

The CRA's *End Child Poverty Week* 2023 focused on five themes: Educational Inequality, Child Protection & Welfare, National Action, Income and Early Years. A fundamental element of the campaign was the series of seminars held by the CRA, helping to boost its call for Budget 2024 to be a children's budget, designed to break the cycle of poverty. As a direct result of the advocacy efforts, a pledge for increased funding was secured, focusing on lobbying for more special needs teachers and higher allowances. To effectively break the cycle of poverty, it was emphasised that early childhood interventions were crucial and needed to be addressed alongside support for school-aged children.

In Spring 2023, the Department of An Taoiseach formed a Child Poverty & Wellbeing Unit based on the CRA reports. This initiative was the government's response to providing the much-needed leadership in tackling child poverty and fostering children's well-being. A Programme Plan is in place for Child Poverty & Well-being from 2023 to 2025, enabling the unit to focus on six critical areas for early action, which bring together policies and services to make a real impact on the lives of children living in poverty, starting with Budget 2024. The annual budget is crucial when the government outlines its priorities for the coming year. Given the government's commitment to reducing child poverty, this unit will ensure that the budget reflects the ambition to improve the lives of children.

On the education front, an extra €21 million allocation in capitation funding (an amount of money given to an organisation for each enrolled pupil by the government) was secured. This will provide much-needed support for primary and secondary schools. The CRA's advocacy efforts led directly to an increased investment in Tusla Education Support Service (TESS). These funds will provide essential provisions such as additional Educational Welfare Officers and more support for interventions like the School Completion Programme, which will benefit children facing educational disadvantage. The Alliance's Spotlight Solution in Education looks closer at the Home School Liaison Programme, which is being extended for the first time to support Traveller and Roma Children in non-DEIS schools. There was an increase in the number of babies receiving their developmental screening checks, from 53.6% in 2021 to 83.3% in 2022. This is a slow return to pre-pandemic levels of public health nurse visits to families in the first year of a child's life. The CRA has been collecting information and actively lobbied for this kind of backing from the government.

This year's *End of Poverty Week* differed from previous campaigns by placing a new emphasis on Early Years. This focus manifested in the introduction of the Home Visitor programme, a new initiative funded to improve communication and connection between children and their families through home visits. The goal is to guide parents through the early stages of raising a family; this early intervention supports parent-child bonding and infant wellbeing, which delivers positive development outcomes. A proposal to improve subsidies, alongside plans to open up the National Childcare Scheme to Child Minders in the National Action Plan for Childminding Improvement, are future goals for the CRA.

Looking at the statistics of single-adult households with children having a higher rate of child poverty of 23.8% *versus* those in two-adult households of 13.1%, these supports will provide essential childcare to single parents experiencing financial distress. This two-way communications strategy fostered mutually beneficial dialogue between the Taoiseach's Office and the public, which helped raise awareness and gather support for struggling families.

The fight for children's well-being took centre stage in the run-up to Budget 2024. The CRA advocated a crucial measure: extending child benefit payments (or an equivalent) to children living in Direct Provision. While this was not implemented directly, the government recognised the success of the DEIS program, which supports disadvantaged schools. Taking a cue from this, the CRA called for a similar model in early years care. This resonated with policymakers, leading to a €4.5 million allocation in Budget 2024 for a new Equal Participation programme that will ensure all children and families have access to the resources they need in their early years.

Despite the financial strain caused by Covid-19 and the Ukraine crisis, securing early childhood funding was a substantial advocacy victory. The organisation achieved a €1 billion commitment, five years ahead of schedule. Core funding will provide the essential foundation for early childhood services. Tackling the disadvantaged, funding will specifically target resources to support children from poor neighbourhoods. Most financial resources will be dedicated to National Childcare and Early Childhood Care & Education (ECCE) programmes – initiatives designed to nurture young minds. The ECCE programme offers free preschool education to all children. The Access & Inclusion Model (AIM) ensures that children with disabilities have equal access to ECCE. The National Child Care Scheme (NCS) makes childcare more affordable for families.

Critical Analysis

A child living in poverty has limited or no access to essentials like healthcare, housing, education and food. It is clear from the work of the CRA that eradicating poverty requires informed political decisions; therefore, it can be alleviated through the proactive advocacy of sustainable policy decisions. The government needs to be transparent in delivering its SDG 1 targets. The OCO goes some way to bridge this gap through its advice and complaints procedures in consultation with members of the public and the Government, but it is the constant advocacy and scrutiny of organisations like the CRA that are most impactful in holding officials to account. The *End Child Poverty* campaigns are well-organised, focused and feature strong panels of experts from academia, civic society, state agencies and senior civil servants. This gives legitimacy to the CRA, which ensures the government listens to and incorporates directly recommendations from this campaign to enhance children's lives.

The CRA's *End Child Poverty Week* was a success in terms of public relations strategy. The event was meticulously organised, showcasing the critical role of effective management in a successful PR campaign. CRA executives demonstrated their leadership by both organising the seminar and participating as panellists. Notably, Tanya Ward, CRA's Chief Executive, was prominent on the panel. The seminar was a prime example of integrated communication functions within an organisation. By focusing on communication, CRA created a two-way symmetrical dialogue model. This model fostered open communication between the audience, the expert panel, and government representatives, establishing a mutually beneficial relationship between CRA and the government. The free exchange of ideas and insights enriched the discussion and strengthened the CRA's advocacy efforts.

Situational theory offers a fresh perspective on the campaign: people are rational, actively seek information, and react based on their circumstances. In other words, context matters. This is evident in four key ways in this campaign: recognising the problem, identifying limitations, getting involved, and gathering information. For instance, the *End Child Poverty Week* seminars identify child poverty as a pressing issue, prompting everyone to brainstorm solutions for the government. Funding constraints are openly acknowledged by the CRA and panellists, urging government action. The seminar's five-day format fosters active involvement and knowledge sharing. By immersing participants in facts and figures, the seminar equips the government with the information needed to combat child poverty in Ireland.

The strategic communications throughout the event embodied the 7Cs of communication (credibility, context, content, clarity, continuity, channels, and capability), making a powerful impact on everyone involved. The speakers' clear, concise messages cut through the noise, leaving no room for misunderstanding. Concrete evidence and research backed their claims, proving that breaking the poverty cycle is possible. The coherent discussions vividly depicted the problem and inspired hope for change. A comprehensive action plan was laid out, offering tangible solutions for impoverished families. A courteous and respectful atmosphere fostered meaningful dialogue and collaboration.

The seminar united influential organisations like Tusla, CRA, and the Taoiseach's Office, breaking them into smaller panels to foster intimate discussions and raise awareness about child poverty. This collaborative research effort aims to galvanise government action, aligning with situational theory's emphasis on information's power to drive change. The hashtag *#EndChildPovertyWeek* serves as a virtual rallying cry, connecting with a broader audience beyond the event itself. Increased awareness can inspire donations and ignite a passion for the cause. After all, breaking the poverty cycle requires resources, and the compelling evidence showcased during the campaign helps steer the government towards achieving SDG 1's ambitious targets.

Conclusion

Ireland's poverty levels have consistently risen over the past decade, with 70,000 more people facing hardship in 2022 compared to 2021. As a signatory of the EU *Child Guarantee*, Ireland is committed to ensuring every child's access to fundamental rights like healthcare, housing, and education. However, challenges such as educational inequality, child welfare concerns, and limited income pose significant barriers for children living in poverty. By thoroughly examining these issues, government officials can develop targeted solutions. This, in turn, could lead to increased funding allocations in the annual budget, effectively breaking the cycle of poverty and contributing to achieving the United Nations' Global Goals. Ireland already boasts the best consultation structures for children in Europe, demonstrating its commitment to addressing their needs. The Irish government, alongside agencies like the OCO and CRA, are actively working to gather data and alleviate child poverty. The 2023 *End Child Poverty Week* shed light on these issues, offering actionable solutions for the government to implement. With a focus on transparency and a substantial financial commitment in the 2024 budget, there is renewed hope for progress in tackling child poverty.

Explorations

1. How did the CRA leverage its communications and PR efforts to help achieve their organisational goals and align with excellence theory?

2. The two-way symmetrical model emphasises dialogue and mutual understanding. How did the CRA go beyond just talking at people during *End Child Poverty Week*?

3. People and organisations react to issues in various ways. What factors influenced how different groups responded to *End Child Poverty Week*?

4. Considering the 7Cs of communication (credibility, context, content, clarity, continuity, channels, and capability), which of these did the CRA use most effectively in this case study?

5. How did the CRA put situational theory into practice during *End Child Poverty Week*?

II. SDG 2 – Zero Hunger
The Grow It Yourself Movement
Avice Meya

Abstract

The Grow It Yourself (GIY) movement, founded by Michael Kelly in 2008, has emerged as a powerful force addressing global challenges in the broken food system. Aligned with SDG 2 – Zero Hunger, GIY promotes sustainable food practices and education through mass food growing programmes. With a focus on inclusivity, accessibility, and partnerships, the movement engages millions in food growing, emphasising individual empowerment and a holistic approach to SDGs. GIY's commitment to continuous improvement positions it as a resilient and impactful contributor to a more sustainable, equitable global food system by 2030.

Introduction

Initiated by Michael Kelly, the Grow It Yourself movement took root with a gathering of 100 people at its inaugural meeting in his hometown of Waterford in 2008. Quickly gaining momentum, this grassroots initiative blossomed into a nationwide phenomenon, cultivating GIY groups throughout Ireland. United by a commitment to sustainable food practices, these communities became hubs of knowledge and action. Kelly's vision transcended mere gardening; it sparked a collective movement redefining the relationship between individuals and their food sources.

In the era of globalised supply chains, GIY emerged as a beacon, challenging the disconnect between consumers and local agriculture. By fostering a sense of community and self-sufficiency, GIY not only encourages the cultivation of sustainable habits but also signifies a broader shift towards a more conscious and resilient approach to food systems. The lack of accessible resources and community support hinders the efforts of people who want to grow food sustainably. This dilemma reflects a broader concern: the disconnect between consumers and the sources of their sustenance. It fosters dependence on distant suppliers and jeopardises local agricultural resilience. As communities struggle with a loss of self-sufficiency, the inception of GIY emphasises the need for localised, community-driven solutions to reimagine and revitalise sustainable food systems. GIY is dedicated to promoting food sustainability and education through food-growing programmes. Its programmes are designed to support mass food growing and embed food sustainability into education systems and community structures. In 2021 alone, over 1 million people participated in a GIY programme or campaign.

Partnering with the Sustainable Development Goals Advocacy Hub, GIY aligns with SDG 2, whose goal is to address the complex challenges within global food systems. The key targets of this goal include eliminating hunger, ensuring access to safe and nutritious food, promoting sustainable agricultural practices, supporting small-scale farmers, and enhancing resilience to climate-related shocks. By partnering with the SDG Advocacy Hub, GIY actively contributes to the global effort to achieve these targets. This emphasises the critical role of local, community-driven initiatives in building a sustainable and resilient food future for all.

Background

Grow It Yourself (GIY) was founded when Michael Kelly, a journalist by profession, had a moment of realisation while shopping in a supermarket in Waterford, Ireland: he discovered that the garlic he was about to buy was imported from China. This led him to start growing his own. However, he soon discovered that he was not good at it and went in search of a local food growers' group where he could learn from experts and meet like-minded people. Finding that there was no such group, Michael decided to create one. At the first meeting of GIY Waterford, 100 people showed up, and the group continued to meet monthly in the city. Then the Waterford GIYers helped start GIY groups in other towns all over Ireland: the idea quickly spread to include hundreds of groups throughout Ireland, and GIY now exists as an international programme. GIY has the ambition to help 4 million people grow some of their food by 2025, and supports people around the world to live healthier, happier, and more sustainable lives. At the core of its endeavours is the concept of food empathy, as it speaks to the changes in knowledge, attitude, and behaviours that happen when people start to grow some of their food. For Kelly, there is a profound optimism in placing a seed in soil in the hope it will someday provide food.

Tactics & Activities

The GIY mission goes beyond mere instruction and advice, which all too easily can be reduced to one-way communication. GIY, as catalysts for change, empowers individuals to recognise the profound impact of their actions on personal health and planetary well-being. The organisation drives audiences in Ireland and abroad toward a more sustainable future through education, advocacy, and community engagement. Alignment with the SDGs is generated through their owned communication channels, partnerships, and practice-based initiatives, making the SDGs relevant and relatable to individuals. Far from being a concept that is vague or misunderstood, sustainability is presented to individuals as something tangible and personally achievable. Rather than negative messaging about what not to do, GIY demonstrates to audiences how their personal actions can contribute to broader global goals. Through social media, webinars, and partnerships with international collaborators, GIY amplifies the message of sustainability and inspiring action at every turn.

GIY believes in practising what it preaches when it comes to sustainable food practices. The organisation is actively involved in various initiatives aimed at promoting a culture of food sustainability in schools and communities. Its most prominent initiative is the 'Grow Cook Eat' kit box, symbolising its commitment to food education and sustainability. More than a box of seeds and soil, it is a powerful tool designed to educate, inspire, and empower individuals to adopt a greener lifestyle. With a simple, inclusive registration process, anyone from households to entire communities can easily sign up for a GROWBox starter kit. These kits comprise 32 compostable pots, 32 'magic' compost discs and an expert GIY resource booklet with growing guides and lessons designed to make food growing accessible to beginners. This is a participatory form of communication: with just a few clicks or scans, the message of sustainability is not only accessed but acted on by the participant. The impact does not end with distribution. The organisation maintains open channels of communication via its website and a custom-devised app to provide plant-growing advice and sustainability tips to help individuals make informed choices. The app builds an interactive community; through monthly webinars and advice sessions, it fosters a vibrant community of knowledge exchange and empowerment, allowing individuals to take meaningful action toward sustainability as part of a collective.

Among its more high-profile activities, GIY worked with RTÉ, Ireland's national broadcaster, to produce a television series about food growth. Over 21 episodes in three seasons from 2019 to 2020, the show, *Grow Cook Eat*, featured Kelly, co-presenter Karen O'Donoghue and professional chefs as they offered straightforward guidance on bringing a different vegetable in each episode from seed to the table. Although the goal of the show was to provide comprehensive assistance to individuals who in Ireland had purchased the GROWBox kit, and stimulate interest in the latent public who had not yet done so, the fact that the show was filmed on location against scenic Irish backdrops resulted in the show being picked up by Amazon Prime, which helped it reach a global audience of 12 million viewers.

One of the communications strengths of GIY is that its activities are informed by research. Its studies have revealed that, when people grow their own food and understand the food system, their knowledge, attitudes, and behaviours around food and the environment shift fundamentally. This shift leads to five fundamental behavioural and attitudinal changes: GIY participants tend to be better at reducing food waste and plastic pollution; they are more likely to increase their consumption of plant-based food, and to shop from local food suppliers, meaning that their food is more sustainable and supports local employment; and they also report feeling a greater connection with the seasons.

It is also more than simply a movement that supports like-minded individuals. It has developed as a strong advocacy organisation, working with other advocacy bodies and private and public sector partners to embed food growth in education systems, led at the national policy level. GIY collaborates with a wide range of partners, including educational institutions such as schools and universities, community organisations such as local gardening clubs and environmental not-for-profit organisations, private sector entities like sustainable agriculture businesses and food producers, and government agencies at local and national levels. These partnerships provide GIY with knowledge and expertise, additional professional resources and networks to access that allows them to advocate sustainable food systems. GIY is, in turn, a member organisation of other organisations and networks, including the Beans Is How coalition, which aims to double the global production and consumption of beans by 2030, and the Chef's Manifesto, a global network of chefs that has devised the SDGs into eight practical themes that professional chefs can integrate into their kitchens.

In cultivating the *GROW at School* food education programme, GIY communications cultivates more than just gardens. Having started with a three-year pilot programme, GIY expanded the *GROW at School* programme nationwide in 2022, with the aim of having one in two primary schools participating. GIY provides a garden kit and lesson plans to help teachers lead students in a journey towards understanding where healthy, sustainable food comes from and transform their awareness of, and attitudes and behaviours towards, food. Again, there are communitarian and participatory aspects visible in this programme: partnerships with educators, parents, and local stakeholders amplify the programme's impact. Together, they sow the seeds of sustainability, fostering curiosity and responsibility in young minds. GIY's *GROW at School* program is not just about growing gardens; it is about nurturing a brighter, greener future for everyone, which is communicated through the schoolchildren's enjoyment and satisfaction of growing their own food.

Results & Outcomes

Despite its genesis predating the SDGs, GIY now fervently champions at least six of these pivotal objectives. At its core, GIY resonates with SDG 2, striving to enhance access to safe, nutritious food, amplify agricultural productivity for small-scale producers, and foster sustainable food production systems. Their endeavours forge a path toward a resilient food supply, resilient in the face of climate upheaval and global crises. Waterford, Kelly's hometown, serves as the nucleus of GIY's operations and is home to GROW HQ, a multipurpose venue comprising a café, cookery school and food growing academy with in-person and online courses.

Communication is the lifeblood of GIY's impact. By rendering food cultivation relevant and accessible, GIY inspires action. Through strategic partnerships and a multimedia approach spanning social platforms, YouTube, and even national TV exposure, GIY amplifies its message to millions. Its presence in esteemed publications and as a nominee for the prestigious international Elevate Prize cements its status as a trailblazer in global food system transformation. Yet, GIY's journey extends beyond online impressions and advertising opportunities as the organisation measures its impact meticulously. GIY ensures its endeavours yield tangible results by scrutinising food-growing behaviours and programme engagement. With aspirations to engage 100 million people by 2030, GIY remains resolute in cultivating a sustainable future for all.

GIY has successfully engaged in over 185 primary schools across Ireland, integrating food-growing education into school curriculums. Over 40,000 children have participated in GIY programmes, learning essential skills and fostering a deeper connection with their food sources. The campaign hopes to target over 100,000 children by the end of 2024. The GROWBox starter kits have seen widespread adoption. To date, GIY has distributed over 50,000 kits, which provide all the necessary materials and instructions to start growing food at home, significantly lowering the barriers to entry for aspiring gardeners.

GIY's campus sites, including the GROW HQ in Waterford, serve as practical examples of sustainable food systems. These sites attract thousands of visitors annually and provide hands-on education through courses and workshops. They also demonstrate the viability of closed-loop systems and zero-waste practices, reinforcing GIY's message and mission. GIY offers courses at its cookery schools and food-growing academies, both online and in-person. These courses cover topics ranging from zero-waste cooking to advanced gardening techniques. Over 10,000 people have participated in these courses, gaining valuable skills and knowledge that they can apply in their daily lives to promote sustainable living.

Through its various programmes, educational resources, and campus location, GIY engages over 1 million people annually. The movement's reach extends beyond Ireland, with programmes and initiatives also being implemented in the UK, USA, and other European regions. GIY's efforts contribute to achieving SDGs, particularly SDG 2 – Zero Hunger, SDG 3 – Good Health & Well-being, SDG 8 – Decent Work & Economic Growth, SDG 12 – Responsible Production & Consumption, SDG 13 – Climate Action, and SDG 15 – Life on Land. Overall, GIY's measurable impact includes widespread educational outreach, substantial GROWBox kit distribution, extensive participation in courses, and significant media engagement, all contributing to a more sustainable and food-secure future.

Critical Analysis

The Grow It Yourself movement emerged as a response to critical issues within the global food system. The movement primarily aimed to address the broken food system, the disconnection between food production and consumption, and the diminishing skill of growing food among the current generation. As the movement evolved, it became evident that it aligned with the conceptual space that eventually became SDG 2 – Zero Hunger, although the SDGs did not exist at the time of movement's inception.

One of the strengths of the GIY movement lies in its clear identification of critical issues, particularly the unsustainable nature of the global food system, and the publics that are not only impacted by them but are open to communication and have transformative potential – like schoolchildren. By highlighting the environmental impact, including the contribution to climate change and the strain on freshwater resources, GIY effectively contextualises its mission within the broader challenges facing the planet. This connection between individual actions and global issues is crucial for mobilising people toward sustainable practices.

The movement's evolution to support multiple SDGs is commendable, and its commitment to addressing issues beyond hunger, such as health, economic growth, responsible production, climate action, and biodiversity, showcases a holistic approach. The emphasis on individual empowerment through food growth as a powerful action is a compelling narrative that resonates with the broader goals of sustainable development. The decision to focus on accessibility and inclusivity is a notable successful communications strategy, positioning food growing as a skill for everyone to enjoy. By reimagining small spaces and removing barriers to participation, GIY has succeeded in making food growing relatable and achievable. This approach aligns with the principles of the SDGs, particularly the aim of leaving no one behind. Additionally, the emphasis on partnerships and collaborations with international organisations enhances the movement's reach and impact.

The use of various communication channels, including social media and a dedicated podcast, demonstrates a contemporary and multifaceted approach to disseminating information. The creation of educational resources, online courses, and physical locations like GROW HQ contributes to a comprehensive strategy for engaging diverse audiences. National awareness campaigns, such as TV shows, have significantly contributed to GIY's reach, allowing it to connect with millions of viewers.

However, despite these strengths, there are areas where the communication of SDG 2 could be enhanced. There is room for more significant alignment and integration with other goals. Integrating the specific targets of SDG2 into the movement's narrative and outcomes would provide a clearer framework for measuring impact and assessing contributions toward achieving Zero Hunger. The movement could explore more targeted communication strategies for engaging with marginalised or vulnerable populations. While it is aware of the additional food security challenges disadvantaged individuals and groups face, a specific focus on tailored communications programmes for them could amplify the movement's impact on social equity.

Another area for improvement lies in the measurement of impact. While the movement highlights engagement metrics, qualitative analysis, and potential yield and CO_2 impact, a more structured and standardised approach to impact assessment would enhance credibility. Collaborating with academic partners is a positive step, and developing a comprehensive impact assessment framework aligned with SDG indicators would further strengthen the movement's accountability. Trust is critical in contemporary strategic communications, and being able to communicate how its activities build trust would enhance its already positive reputation.

The GIY movement has made significant strides in promoting sustainable food practices and aligning with the principles of SDG 2. Its commitment to inclusivity, accessibility, and individual empowerment is commendable. However, a more explicit integration of SDG 2 targets, enhanced impact measurement practices, and targeted strategies for vulnerable populations would further strengthen its effectiveness in contributing to a more sustainable and equitable food system.

Conclusions

In conclusion, the GIY movement is a noteworthy force in sustainable food practices, successfully addressing critical global challenges associated with the broken food system. By fostering a deep connection between individual actions and broader environmental and societal issues, GIY has effectively communicated its mission and engaged millions in the food-growing journey. The movement's evolution to support multiple SDGs, particularly SDG 2, showcases a holistic and impactful approach. While the movement has demonstrated considerable strengths, including inclusivity, accessibility, and collaborative partnerships, there are areas for refinement. A more explicit incorporation of SDG 2 targets into the movement's narrative and a standardised impact assessment framework would enhance its credibility and contribute to a more comprehensive understanding of its contributions.

Additionally, targeted strategies for engaging marginalised populations could further amplify GIY's positive impact on social equity. As GIY continues to inspire individuals globally to embark on their food-growing and food empathy journeys, the movement's longevity and adaptability reflect its resilience. With a commitment to continuous improvement, the GIY movement has the potential to not only meet its ambitious targets but also contribute significantly to a more sustainable, equitable, and resilient global food system by 2030.

Explorations

1. How important is the participatory aspect of the Grow It Yourself movement as a form of public relations?

2. What are the challenges of focusing strategic communications campaigns through schools?

3. What other community or community of interest groups could Grow It Yourself address to spread its message?

4. Owned channels of communication are important in this campaign. How might Grow It Yourself achieve better earned coverage?

5. What storytelling techniques could be used to tailor Grow It Yourself to different audiences?

III. SDG 3 – Good Health & Well-being
Alcohol Action Ireland & Minimum Unit Pricing

Eve Wright

Abstract

This case study analyses Alcohol Action Ireland's campaign to implement Minimum Unit Pricing (MUP) in Ireland, a decade after it was first proposed, and how implementing MUP and other measures intended to reduce alcohol harm impacts the SDGs. SDG Target 3.5 seeks to reduce the harm caused by alcohol and strengthen the prevention and treatment of substance abuse. Alcohol misuse poses a significant public health challenge in Ireland, costing the State around €1.9 billion in health-related costs and claiming over 1,540 lives every year. In 2018, the *Public Health (Alcohol) Act* was enacted in Ireland to address alcohol misuse, recommending minimum unit pricing as one of the measures to reduce alcohol harm.

Introduction

In Ireland, alcohol use causes over 1,540 deaths annually and incurs around €1.9 billion in health-related costs. It is estimated that 15% of the adult population have an alcohol use disorder. Harmful use of alcohol is drinking that has serious negative health and social affects for drinkers, the people around drinkers such as families, friends and colleagues, and society. Patterns of drinking, such as binge drinking, are also associated with increased misuse. Not only does alcohol impact the individuals who consume it, but third parties are often negatively impacted by the misuse of alcohol by others. It increases the risk of a person committing violence against another and is a leading cause of fatal road traffic accidents. Children are also negatively impacted by the alcohol use of their parents through foetal alcohol syndrome and disorders in the family home.

According to the World Health Organisation (WHO), alcohol use adversely impacts 13 of the 17 SDGs and 32 Targets. Alcohol is addressed explicitly by Target 3.5, which seeks to reduce the harm caused by alcohol and strengthen the prevention and treatment of substance abuse, including harmful alcohol use. However, alcohol use contributes to poverty, violence against women and girls, child abuse, and decreased economic productivity. By reducing the harm caused by alcohol, progress will be made towards achieving better health, and many other goals will be positively impacted.

Alcohol Action Ireland (AAI) is a national independent advocate for reducing alcohol harm in Ireland. Established in 2003, AAI has campaigned for action to be taken by the State and public health organisations to reduce the harm caused by alcohol misuse and to raise awareness of alcohol-related harm. Under WHO guidance, the alcohol industry should have no role in formulating alcohol policies, which must be kept free from lobbying by or influence from commercial organisations and other vested interests. AAI does not work with the drinks industry or its funded groups.

One such campaign led by AAI was the Minimum Unit Pricing (MUP) campaign. First proposed by AAI in 2012, MUP was implemented by the government in May 2021 and commenced in January 2022, after nearly a decade of campaigning and lobbying by AAI. MUP is one of the strategies recommended by WHO to reduce alcohol harm. In countries where MUP has been implemented, there has been a measurable decrease in alcohol harm.

Background

In 2012, the Department of Health published a *Steering Group Report on National Substance Misuse Strategy*. It put forward several measures to address the high levels of alcohol misuse in Ireland. One of the recommended measures was the implementation of MUP. The report recommended that a minimum price be set for alcoholic drinks, based on the number of grams of alcohol in a drink. Also recommended in this report were measures that would legislate the marketing and availability of alcohol to consumers. The MUP recommended by the Steering Group was that a standard drink containing 10g of alcohol could not be sold for less than €1.

One of the reasons MUP is so effective at reducing alcohol harm is that it increases the price of the cheapest drinks, and heavy alcohol users typically favour more affordable drinks. Moderate drinkers do not tend to purchase the cheapest alcohol available. Therefore, MUP targets price increases at at-risk drinkers and not those who consume low to moderate amounts of alcohol. AAI conducted annual price surveys which showed that standard drinks were available to Irish consumers for under €1, with spirits like vodka being available for €0.63c. An OECD report published in 2021 revealed that Ireland had the second most affordable alcohol index among OECD members.

There is compelling evidence to support the effectiveness of MUP from both studies in Canadian provinces and modelling studies across various countries. Evaluation studies in Canada revealed that increasing MUP levels correlated with reduced alcohol consumption, decreased alcohol-related hospital admissions, and fewer alcohol-related traffic offences. Modelling studies across the UK, Ireland, Australia, and Germany consistently show that MUP is highly effective in reducing alcohol-related deaths, criminal offences, hospital admissions, and workplace absences. Emerging evidence from Scotland, which implemented MUP in 2018, further supports the positive impact of MUP on reducing alcohol harm.

MUP and other proposals from the Steering Group Report were included in legislation passed in 2018 as the *Public Health (Alcohol) Act* (PHAA). However, MUP was not implemented as it was outlined that it should be brought in at the same time MUP was being implemented in Northern Ireland. Due to the Northern Ireland Assembly being suspended from 2017 to 2020, more progress was needed in implementing the measure. Therefore, AAI began an advocacy campaign to push for the implementation of MUP in Ireland.

The AAI and the Royal College of Physicians in Ireland established the Alcohol Health Alliance Ireland in 2015. It was the first public health lobbying group to support the PHAA. Over 60 other organisations and individuals joined the alliance, including the Irish Cancer Society and the Children's Rights Alliance. Although the work of the Alliance essentially concluded when the PHAA was enacted in October 2018, the AAI encouraged members to support its campaign for the full implementation of MUP, such as by signing important letters to politicians. The AAI also encouraged the public to join its advocacy efforts by devising an online campaign asking the public to contact their elected representatives about MUP.

Tactics & Activities

Because the introduction of MUP required a political decision, politicians were one of the main publics AAI sought to communicate with their campaign. AAI met with key political stakeholders and presented vital evidence for the effectiveness of MUP and polling data that indicated strong public support for the measures included in the PHAA. This was done to ensure that the full implementation of the PHAA was included in the manifestos of all the main political parties in the 2020 General Election. AAI also met with Ministers to ensure that MUP and the PHAA would be raised in the Oireachtas. AAI maintained close contact with policymakers in Northern Ireland throughout the campaign. When the Minister for Health in Northern Ireland announced that it was unlikely that MUP would be introduced in the period of the current Assembly, AAI made the argument that waiting for MUP to be introduced in tandem with Northern Ireland was not acceptable or feasible.

While the Covid-19 pandemic presented challenges to the campaign, it also presented an opportunity for AAI to point out the impact that alcohol was having on the health system. During the pandemic, up to 20% of ICU capacity in some hospitals was being used for alcohol-related health problems. Staff at Beaumont Hospital reported that one in every five patients admitted to critical care was an alcohol-related admission. This highlighted how alcohol added strain to the public health system at a time when hospitals were under immense pressure.

One of the challenges AAI faced in their political advocacy was the drink industry's access to politicians. The PHAA has been described as one of the most contested pieces of legislation in the history of the State. According to the Lobbying Register, the drinks industry gained access to senior politicians and TDs 361 times since the proposal of the PHAA. AAI did not have the resources to access politicians at the same rate. The influence of the drinks industry on Irish society is one of the main challenges AAI faces in its advocacy, even beyond campaigning for MUP. The industry has much influence on conversations about alcohol misuse in Ireland. Even Drinkaware, a national organisation with charitable status that seeks to prevent and reduce alcohol misuse, receives funding from the drinks industry, such as Diageo and Bulmers Ireland, which presents a significant conflict of interest.

Communicating accurate information about MUP was essential to harnessing support from the public. Through its website and social media communications, AAI stressed that MUP would have little to no impact on low-risk drinkers but would reduce the harm by targeting the cheapest and strongest drinks. Social media graphics were created and distributed, showing how little a man or woman can spend to meet their low-risk weekly drinking limit. A significant aspect of the campaign was the sharing of personal testimony. *David's Story* was a heart-rending video featuring John Higgins sharing the story of his son David, who died by suicide, with alcohol being a contributing factor. The video, which has been viewed over 60,000 times, not only shares David's story but highlights the relationship between alcohol, mental health, and suicide. Throughout the campaign, AAI issued multiple press releases and reports, having 641 contributions to broadcast, press, and online news items in 2021, the year the government announced MUP would be introduced in Ireland.

Results

In January 2022, MUP was implemented across the country. A minimum price of 10c per gram of alcohol was set. Minister for Health Stephen Donnelly TD said that the measure was intended to reduce serious illness and death from alcohol misuse, while it would also alleviate pressure on public health services from alcohol-related conditions. He referenced how the measure had proven successful in Scotland. In the lead-up to MUP being implemented, AAI began an awareness campaign to inform the public about what the measure would entail. MUP faced criticism in the media, with some calling it a tax on people with low incomes and the working class and questioning its efficacy. AAI's awareness campaign worked to defend the measure against criticism and continued to point towards research supporting MUP's efficacy.

As only two years have passed since the implementation of MUP, it is difficult to judge the measure's efficacy accurately and whether it has contributed to a reduction in alcohol misuse. In 2022, the Revenue Commissioners reported that alcohol consumption increased. However, this may be attributed to the reopening of the hospitality sector following the Covid-19 pandemic. AAI reported that in the first year of MUP being implemented, alcohol consumption declined by 5% compared with pre-pandemic use in 2019. The fact that Northern Ireland has not implemented MUP may also present challenges for proving the efficacy of MUP in reducing alcohol harm, as off-licences in the North reported an increase in customers from Ireland travelling to purchase alcohol at a cheaper price. This was one of the concerns raised by Drinks Ireland, the industry body, about MUP, who feared it might put pressure on border businesses and increase illegal alcohol smuggling. This is one reason why the WHO recommended that regions collaborate on alcohol policies. The positive impact of MUP remains to be seen. However, evidence from Scotland, which has had MUP in place since 2018, indicates that MUP is effective at reducing alcohol harm, and AAI is hopeful that this will be mirrored in Ireland over the coming years.

Critical Analysis

AAI's campaign to implement MUP in Ireland can be considered a success because MUP is now in place. It can also be considered a successful promotion of the SDGs and demonstrates how SDGs can be promoted and advocated for in advocacy and lobbying. However, it can be argued that the campaign's success is measured not only by the policy being enacted but also by the mission of the organisation being furthered. Therefore, to thoroughly examine the campaign's success, a better indication of MUP's impact on alcohol misuse in Ireland is necessary. However, this will not be possible until adequate time has passed with MUP being in place. However, some commentary can be offered on the campaign's success, considering the impact MUP has made over the first two years of its implementation.

AAI was up against a formidable force: the drinks industry strongly influences many aspects of Irish society, including the media. Especially in the lead-up to MUP's implementation in January 2022, the media challenged the measure, particularly for being seen as targeting working-class and low-income consumers. The efficacy of MUP continues to be questioned by the media, which points out that alcohol consumption has not decreased since its implementation. The issue of Northern Ireland not having MUP has also been a media talking point, especially as this was one of the major concerns of MUP's critics before its implementation. This issue brings into question the decision to push for MUP in Ireland without waiting for Northern Ireland to implement it in tandem. This highlights the need for the SDGs to be indeed global and ensure nations collaborate to reach targets and indicators together.

Despite this, AAI made skilful use of political advocacy in this campaign and showed the role lobbying can play in promoting the SDGs. As it is a public health lobbying group and MUP required a political decision, focusing its efforts on contacting politicians and ministers was wise. Although AAI did not have the same access to senior politicians and TDs that lobbyists in the drinks industry did, they were able to collaborate with other organisations in the AHAI to increase their influence and encourage the public to contact politicians regarding the issue as well. The campaign's response to the Covid-19 pandemic was both opportunistic and informative. AAI used the pandemic's spotlight on healthcare strains to draw attention to the substantial burden that alcohol-related health problems placed on the system. This tactic underscored the urgency of implementing MUP and demonstrated the campaign's adaptability in navigating unforeseen challenges. The use of personal testimony in their communications through the *David's Story* video was compelling and made the issue AAI sought to address more personal. In addition to the facts and figures being presented, this was important to demonstrate the impact of MUP on alcohol misuse in Ireland.

While this campaign directly addressed SDG Target 3.5, alcohol harm adversely impacts 13 of the 17 SGDs. Not only does a measure like MUP advance Target 3.5 in reducing alcohol misuse, but it will positively impact other areas of society. Although critics of MUP claimed it was unfairly targeting people experiencing poverty, WHO reports that alcohol increases inequalities between and within countries and that individuals and families affected by alcohol misuse are more vulnerable to poverty and food insecurity. This campaign and its goals demonstrate how SDGs can be interconnected and how addressing one target can also lead to positive progress towards other targets.

Conclusion

The realisation of the MUP campaign by AAI stands as a pivotal achievement in the ongoing battle against the severe consequences of alcohol misuse in Ireland. With over 1,540 annual alcohol-related deaths and staggering health-related costs of approximately €1.9 billion, the imperative for effective measures is indisputable. AAI's commitment to advocating for policies prioritising public health over commercial interests has guided its impactful journey. The road to MUP's implementation was fraught with challenges, including delays due to the suspended Northern Ireland Assembly. Undeterred, AAI launched a strategic advocacy campaign, effectively engaging with key political stakeholders and ministers to ensure MUP's prominence in political manifestos. The unexpected obstacle presented by the Covid-19 pandemic became an opportunity for AAI to emphasise the strain on the healthcare system due to alcohol-related admissions, highlighting the urgency of MUP implementation and showcasing the campaign's adaptability.

The campaign's alignment with SDG Target 3.5 demonstrates the importance of lobbying in promoting the SDGs. Even though the SDGs were not explicitly mentioned in AAI's media campaigns targeting the public, they still brought awareness to the issues they seek to address. Not only did it address SDG Target 3.5, but as was previously mentioned, it also addressed the numerous other targets and indicators that are also impacted by alcohol harm. As Ireland awaits the unfolding impact of MUP in the coming years, AAI remains hopeful, given the positive outcomes witnessed in Scotland. The campaign provides a template for navigating the complex intersections of health, policy, and societal well-being, setting a precedent for future campaigns in the realm of public health advocacy.

Explorations

1. How did Alcohol Action Ireland leverage political advocacy and stakeholder engagement to promote the implementation of minimum unit pricing? What were the key tactics used to influence political decisionmakers?

2. How did media coverage shape public opinion and policy decisions regarding the *Public Health (Alcohol) Act* and minimum unit pricing?

3. What challenges did AAI face in maintaining consistent and accurate public messaging during the Covid-19 pandemic? How did they adapt their PR strategy to highlight the relevance of minimum unit pricing considering the pandemic's impact on the healthcare system?

4. Consider the role of personal testimony and public awareness campaigns in the AAI's campaign. How effective were they in garnering public and political support?

5. How did AAI counter criticism from the drinks industry and media that minimum unit pricing would unfairly target low-income consumers? What communications strategies were employed to mitigate these concerns?

IV. Intermezzo 1
Communicating the SDGs through Public Relations Paradigms
Isaac Antwi-Boasiako

Introduction

The advent of the 17 SDGs and their various targets designed by the UN in 2015 as universal objectives of achieving a better world by 2030 have been hailed as a milestone step, while critics see it as an over-ambitious project. Nonetheless, the SDGs have come to stay and have been embraced by many countries, NGOs, corporate institutions, and other international bodies. Since its inception, the SDGs framework has been criticised as needing more adequate awareness and promotion among global audiences. For instance, in Ireland, only 12% of the Irish population is aware of the SDGs, and to correct this phenomenon, the Irish government has chosen 26 organisations to champion the country's 2023-2024 SDGs drive of raising awareness and educating the public about the 17 SDGs and their targets (UNRIC, 2024). A study by Odoom *et al.* (2024), which also discusses the SDGs awareness and knowledge in Africa using Ghana as a case study, depicts a low level of public awareness and knowledge about global goals. According to the study, the first six SDGs (Ending Poverty, Zero Hunger, Health & Well-being, Gender Equality, and Clean Water & Sanitation) have a relatively high score of public awareness in Ghana. This study affirms the work of Akinlolu *et al.* (2017) about similar trends in Nigeria.

In Europe, the 2017 *Eurobarometer* report about the awareness and knowledge of the SDGs shows that only 1 in 10 European citizens know and are aware of what the SDGs are (Eurobarometer, 2017). This problem can be attributed to lacking a specific body responsible for the SDGs' PR activities. Many stakeholders have taken responsibility for spreading the SDGs story. However, these attempts have been fragmented and disorganised due to the absence of a central body responsible for the PR aspect of the agenda 2030. The 2019 European Sustainable Development Network (ESDN) report about communication for sustainable development and the SDGs of 70 stakeholders from 17 countries also highlighted the issue of disjointed SDG communications and low public awareness and education (Mulholland, 2019). There may have been an improvement since 2017, but there is more to do regarding designing effective and strategic communication campaigns for the SDGs based on PR paradigms.

Considering the above, this chapter explores the core PR paradigms of effective communication. It argues that public relations paradigms should underpin the production and dissemination of the SDGs' communication messages and strategies. It is virtually impossible to communicate the SDGs effectively and strategically without observing the core principles, assumptions, and scientific worldview established by the public relations discipline. The PR paradigms, such as Excellence and its four models – relationship management, rhetoric, global public relations, and Ubuntu – which are explored in this paper, can provide practical and theoretical foundations and frameworks for effectively establishing SDG communications. The SDGs topic is complex; thus, communicating such issues needs paradigms that can shape and direct the strategic plan and activities. Effective communication for the SDGs must be underpinned by certain paradigms, and the public relations discipline offers diverse paradigms to help shape the strategic communications activities designed by organisations advancing the SDGs. A set of paradigms must back all communication activities, and the global communications goals must be backed by PR strategic management and symbolic-interpretive paradigms. They are general concepts upon which communication practices are founded. The public relations field as a communication discipline is endowed with various paradigms, and PR practices are explained under the lens of these theoretical frameworks. This chapter examines how PR paradigms can improve SDG communications if sustainable development communicators leverage them in their domestic and foreign publics engagements to achieve the UN 2030 agenda. The paper posits that the paradigms intersect with the SDGs, and organisations seeking to include part of the SDGs in their campaigns and mission statements need to value these PR paradigms' essential role in their communication strategies.

PR Paradigms at a Glance

It is important to explore the general paradigms to understand how PR paradigms can serve as the SDGs' communication campaign frameworks. Every academic field uses paradigms and theories to help understand and conduct its research. Public Relations as an applied and academic field equally uses paradigms to help understand how public relations is practiced and how this practice can be improved for organisations, society, and the publics (Brunner, 2019; Grunig, 2008; Grunig et al., 2006). Steyn's (2004) work on paradigm application to the PR field explains why paradigms should be applied to the public relations communication practices from Kuhn's (1970) paradigm theory perspective. Some PR scholars, such as Toth and Dozier, argue that "executing effective public relations starts with knowing and understanding the public relations [paradigms] that help define the practice" (Brunner, 2019).

A paradigm can be defined as a cohort of researchers with similar scientific worldviews, interests, and assumptions pursuing similar scholarly research with similar methods and approaches (Zhou, 2022). It can also be described as a set of assumptions, theories, and models commonly accepted by scholars in a particular academic discipline (Steyn, 2004). The PR paradigm can be broadly classified into functional, interpretive, and critical paradigms (see Toth & Heath, 1992; Zhou *et al.*, 2022). However, two main competing PR paradigms exist: the strategic management behavioural paradigm and the symbolic-interpretive paradigm (Grunig, 2009). Many other contrasting PR paradigms and struggles also exist. For instance, the work of Zhou *et al.* (2022) on the evolution of 'PR paradigmatism' between 2010 and 2020 identified nine paradigms commonly associated with PR discipline within that decade: strategic management, PR professionalism, digital media, crisis communication, internal communication, global public relations, media relations, rhetoric and philosophy, and critical studies. Although scholars and practitioners may not agree on the best paradigm or approach, they may agree that PR paradigms are needed to understand better certain aspects of PR practices, such as crisis and issue communications, global audience engagements, media relations, etc (Brunner, 2019). They all aim to improve PR communication practices.

The functional or strategic management paradigm provides frameworks for organisational and management aspects of PR above message-centred communications. This paradigm has dominated the PR field for decades until the advent of the interpretive and critical paradigms – the postmodernists (Rubtcova & Pavenkov, 2019; Verwey, 2015). However, Steyn (2004) sees persuasion as the dominant paradigm of PR. Public relations theories under the functional or strategic management paradigm include Excellence and its models, relationship management, and situational theories. These are classified as the modernist paradigms. This PR paradigm aims to advance a behavioural, managerial model in which communication management becomes the critical function of PR practitioners. It sees PR as a "participant in organisational decisionmaking instead of a conveyor of messages about decisions made by other managers" (Grunig, 2009). This conception of PR leads the paradigm advocates to approach the discipline as a research-based approach mechanism for organisational listening and learning.

The interpretive PR paradigm is based on message-centred and meaning in PR communication. It puts reputation, messaging, persuasion, perception, media relations, publicity, and brands as key functions of PR. The corporate sustainability communication concept (Signitzer & Prexl, 2007) also falls within this paradigm. It asserts that publics can be persuaded and thus sees persuasion as a key function of the PR discipline. These paradigms argue that publics' cognitions, behaviours, and attitudes can be swayed and influenced through persuasive communication tactics. The critical PR paradigm, on the contrary, focuses on the critique of the practice of PR practitioners and researchers (Pieczka, 2006).

The next section examines the role of PR paradigms in fostering awareness, education, engagement, and action by organisations and other SDG communicators to achieve the set development goals on a global scale. The paradigms discussed below are from the functional or strategic management and symbolic-interpretive perspectives of PR, and the Ubuntu paradigm is also introduced as a potential communication framework for the PR field and the SDG communication activities.

Functional PR Paradigms: The Grunigian PR Paradigm as the SDGs' Communication Framework

The International Association of Business Communicators sponsorship project of proposed research in 1984 gave birth to what is generally known in public relations as the Excellence theory, headed by James Grunig and his associates (Grunig *et al.*, 2006). Hence, the term 'Grunigian school' or 'Grunigian paradigm'. The paradigm argues that PR has a more excellent value for organisations and society when it is integrated strategically, symmetrically, and managerially. The main goal of the Grunigian paradigm is to answer the question of how and why public relations have value to an organisation. The core of the excellence theory is to "build good long-term relationships with strategic publics" (Heath & Coombs, 2006). It is a general public relations theory that brings together ideas about communication practices within organisations (Grunig, 1993). In other words, the theory focuses on Excellence and effectiveness in public relations practice. It is also normative, since it prescribes how a public relations department should be structured and function (Heath & Coombs, 2006). In this regard, the Excellence theory provides guidelines for establishing an excellent public relations practice. The Grunigian paradigm was developed almost four decades ago, and the PR field has seen a clear paradigm shift from Grunigian thought to more persuasive and critical thinking, with paradigms such as rhetorical theory and critical post-modernism taking centre stage. Also, having one dominant theoretical paradigm in the field raises concerns and many questions; as Botan & Hazleton (2006) note, "scholarly research moves forward by competition between different perspectives".

The Grunigian PR models and the SDG campaigns

The Grunigian theoretical paradigm of Excellence also introduced what has become known as the PR models to explain how and the type of communication activities carried out by organisations to engage their stakeholders. In other words, the four models help to explain PR communication practices. Although various forms of PR models exist, such as mixed-motive, Grunig's four models have been arguably the most contested and often cited in public relations scholarships. These models are the press agentry / publicity, public information, two-way asymmetrical, and two-way symmetrical (Grunig, 1992, 2008, 2009; Grunig & Hunt, 1984).

The first model, the press agentry / publicity, is also known as a one-way communication model (see Grunig & Hunt, 1984). It demands practitioners to "seek attention for the organisation or client almost any way possible" (Grunig et al., 2006). Grunig argues that this model serves as a propagandistic function and can be best described as a craft version of asymmetrical public relations (Grunig, 2008; see also Khattab, 2020). This model is characterised by the use of persuasion and manipulation to influence publics to behave as the organisation wishes (Grunig & Hunt, 1984). Generally, this paradigm advocates for attention generation and public opinion manipulation. In the context of the SDG campaigns, communicators can generate public attention and shape public opinion using communication tactics such as promotional campaigns through social and traditional media, press releases, and staged events. SDG stakeholders can use this paradigm to raise awareness of specific SDGs, highlight their own sustainability initiatives or showcase partnerships with NGOs or governmental agencies, as most of the case studies in this book have been done in Ireland.

The public information model is described as a one-way communication model that requires the practitioner, usually in-house, to distribute truthfully, but mainly only favourable, information. Grunig (1993) again sees this model as the journalistic type of two-way asymmetrical PR. This form of model is also characterised by the use of press releases and other one-way communication tactics to disseminate organisational information (Grunig et al., 1995; Grunig & Hunt, 1984; Khattab, 2020). Examples of institutions that practice this model are NGOs, governments, and state institutions like the police. Campaigners of the SDGs, particularly state institutions and NGOs, can adopt this paradigm in their communication strategies by providing credible and accessible information about the SDGs through press releases and other platforms such as websites and social media, as well as sharing best sustainable development practices. By doing this, organisations enhance public understanding of sustainability issues and empower different stakeholders to take action in support of the SDGs.

The third Grunigian model – the two-way asymmetrical – is a two-way communication model that requires practitioners to "conduct scientific research to determine how to persuade publics to behave in the ways their client organisation wish" (Grunig et al., 1995). Grunig describes this model as the "epitome of much modern, sophisticated public relations practice and a scientific version of public relations practice" (Grunig, 2008). It is a two-way imbalanced communication (Grunig & Hunt, 1984). This model is characterised by the use of persuasion and manipulations to alter the behaviour of its audience to suit the organisational interest. Its research is one-sided since it does not dig into the feelings of its publics toward the organisation (Grunig, 2008; Grunig et al., 2006). Corporate organisations are typical examples of entities that practice this model. This paradigm can provide a framework for framing SDGs in ways that align with organisational goals. Within this framework, SDG communicators can undertake research about their targeted audience and how best to persuade them, as the 2019 ESDN report on SDG communications proposed. Communicators must have an idea of their audience's background.

The fourth model, the two-way symmetrical, is a "public relations model developed to explain a symbiotic relationship between organisations and their publics where communication is developed through research and is often in the form of multidirectional dialogue" (Khattab, 2020). It is the ideal form of communication model, characterised by the use of communication to negotiate with the public, resolve conflicts and promote mutual understanding (Grunig & Hunt, 1984). This fourth model has come under massive criticism by some scholars who argue that it is an ideal and normative model (Khattab, 2020). Others also opined on PR's inherently undemocratic and asymmetric nature (Edwards, 2006; L'Etang, 2009; Pieczka, 2016). Though seen as an idealistic approach, SDG communicators can use this paradigm to engage stakeholders and the targeted publics in meaningful conversations about sustainability challenges and may solicit feedback on organisational practices. I hold that, by adopting this paradigm, stakeholders involved in championing the SDGs can build trust and credibility, which are crucial for successfully implementing the global goals.

All four Grunigian models explain the various approaches communicators adopt to carry out their communication strategies. SDG communicators can combine any of the four paradigms depending on the goal of the communication campaign. Although publicity is the most used paradigm, state institutions, NGOs, and corporate institutions advocating for SDGs may adopt a combination since they are not mutually exclusive.

In summary, the Grunigian Excellence and its four models concept present a strategic management paradigm approach to public relations practice as it attempts to establish the value of public relations at various organisational levels based on system theory (Grunig, 2008; Wakefield, 1997; Yun, 2006). It offers five propositions that theorists believe are common to all organisations with excellent public relations: participative culture, symmetrical internal communication, organic structures, equal employee opportunities, and job satisfaction (Grunig et al., 2006). Grunig and his associates assert that CEOs with excellent PR departments valued communication twice as much as those with less excellent departments, and they also affirmed that PR should function as stipulated in the excellence theory (Grunig, 2008; Grunig & Grunig, 2008).

Regarding the SDGs, the Grunigian paradigm focuses on symmetrical communication, which includes listening to stakeholders, engaging in dialogue, and fostering mutual understanding. PR practitioners involved in the SDGs drives can apply this paradigm's principle to sustainability initiatives by soliciting feedback from different stakeholders, addressing their concerns, and co-creating viable solutions that align with the SDGs. The UN can establish an excellent

PR department for SDG communications based on the Grunigian paradigm. This will fill the lacuna of a responsible PR body to spearhead the SDGs' global awareness, participation, and knowledge. The UN, its Member States, and other stakeholders promulgating the SDGs and their targets through communication should symmetrically and managerially integrate PR into their activities to appreciate PR's excellent value. Organisations championing SDG can build stronger relationships with stakeholders and enhance support for sustainable development efforts by prioritising two-way symmetrical communication and collaborations.

The relationship management paradigm and the SDGs

Relationship management is a general theoretical paradigm of PR, which states that "balancing the interests of organisations and publics is achieved through management of organisation-public relationships" (Ledingham, 2006). From this notion, PR is perceived as the "management function that establishes and maintains mutually beneficial relationships between an organisation and the publics on whose its success or failure depends" (Cutlip, Center & Broom, 1994). This PR paradigm sees management as a central tool in shaping the organisation's public engagement. The management aspect provides a framework for conducting PR campaigns based on planning, implementation, and evaluation. The relational paradigm has been used in various PR functions such as issues and crisis management, community relations, public affairs, and media relations (Ledingham, 2006; Sriramesh, 2009).

The PR paradigm has shifted more from image building to relationship building. Relationships have become one of the central tenets of modern PR. The discipline's emphasis on building and maintaining mutually beneficial relationships is one of the PR's main strengths (Taylor & Kent, 2006). This approach is a means of creating trust and gaining support among the targeted publics. The relationship management PR paradigm shows that public relations plays an important role in building relationships at the international and home levels. The PR is still about an organisation's relationship with its publics, argues Grunig (2009).

The dominant concept of strategic management of relationships in the relationship management paradigm implies that 'managing' means planning, control, feedback, and performance; 'strategic' signifies planning, prioritisation, and action orientation, while 'relationships' means effective and strategic communication, mutual understanding and dependency, trust, commitment and shared responsibility and values (Steyn, 2004). The SDGs' communication campaigns are one vehicle for relationship building. Relationships involve negotiations, trust, and mutual respect for other parties – dialogue. In this regard, SDG communication activities to be carried out by organisations should be flexible and address the diverse needs of the targeted global publics. Under this paradigm, I believe that, by cultivating strong, mutually beneficial relationships with the targeted publics and other stakeholders, organisations involved in promoting the SDGs can leverage their support to drive meaningful change and advance sustainable development goals.

The global public relations paradigm and the SDGs

The global public relations paradigm explores the question of whether PR practices and theory should be unique to each country and culture or whether the same practice should be carried out everywhere. The advocates of this paradigm concluded that global public relations should come between "standardisation and individualisation" (Grunig, 2009). They argue that certain generic PR principles can be practiced globally but, at local levels, they should be applied differently in different situations and locations. It provides six main contextual conditions that global PR practitioners should consider when applying the generic principles: culture, political system, economic system, level of economic development, extent and nature of activism, and media landscape (Sriramesh & Verčič, 2009).

PR scholars such as Wang (2011) explain that a paradigm is supposed to reflect the values and aspirations of the historical, cultural, and social context of the place in which it was developed. This assertion affirms the importance of the global public relations paradigm, where certain PR paradigms developed in Western historical, cultural, and social contexts do not mostly reflect the needs and values of the non-Western environment regarding strategic communication. The global public relations paradigm is essential for SDG communications because sustainability goals are global, transcending cultures and social and political boundaries. PR practitioners advancing the SDGs in different countries should consider the paradigm's six contextual conditions for engaging global audiences.

Interpretive PR Paradigms

Achieving SDGs through the rhetorical PR paradigm

The theoretical paradigm shift in PR is witnessed in the advent of the rhetorical public relations theory, which has been a fierce competitor to the Grunigian paradigm that has dominated the field for many years. The rhetorical school is championed heavily by Robert Heath (1993, 2000, 2005) with his famous quote that "rhetoric is the essence of public relations" (Heath, 1993). In much of his writings, Heath has advocated using rhetorical theory to advance a theoretical comprehension of public relations. He adopted the philosophical concept of the rhetoric of the early Greek philosophers like Aristotle and modern philosopher Kenneth Burke to the public relations field as an alternative to the Excellence theory (Moloney & McGrath, 2020).

The adherents of this school argue that the main reason for applying rhetoric to public relations practice is that "rhetoric is the strategic art of effective public communications" (Heath & Coombs, 2006). People become persuaded by the quality of evidence and reasoning provided to them by speakers or writers, argue Heath & Coombs (2006). The rhetorical public relations approach advocates argue that "public relations is existentially about persuasive communication" (Moloney & McGrath, 2020; Pfau & Wan, 2006); persuasion becomes the main focus of the paradigm. Practitioners of the field use argumentative rhetoric to persuade their targeted publics to accept a particular opinion, behaviour, or action. Good rhetoric is the most credible and persuasive message to the greatest number of its targeted publics.

The basic tenet of the rhetorical public relations theory is the examination of the symbolic exchange of words and visuals in PR messages sent out by organisations and groups to promote their interests in the political economy and civil society to analyse their meanings, their ethics, and their effects (Moloney & McGrath, 2020). The paradigm is concerned with language, words, images, and oral and written narratives, since the core of public relations campaigns are language, messages, image, and virtual narratives (Moloney & McGrath, 2020). As Heath notes, "language is not a tool, but a way of understanding the dynamics of discourse creating shared and competing worldviews that shed light onto the vicissitudes of coordinating social action" (Kent, 2011). The rhetorical PR paradigm can assist organisations in becoming "the good organisation communicating well" (Heath, 2000). It views public relations as "the management function that rhetorically adapts organisations to people's interests and people's interests to organisations by co-creating meaning and co-managing cultures to achieve mutually beneficial relationships" (Heath, 2000). Dialogue is also another essential element of the rhetorical PR paradigm.

The advocates of the SDGs can also use the rhetorical PR paradigm as the foundation for their communication campaigns because national and international public relations comprise persuasive communication and advocacy acts directed at domestic and foreign audiences. The rhetorical PR paradigm also accepts advocacy as one of its primary principles. Foreign and domestic publics engagement by states and non-state actors involves persuasion and advocacy, which are central elements of the rhetorical PR theory. Communication of SDGs can be enhanced when communicators apply this paradigm to identify common ground – identifying shared values and goals between organisations and targeted publics. They can also use storytelling as part of their narrative framing to shape opinions and perceptions. The rhetorical paradigm can also provide a framework for SDGs argumentation and persuasion – using persuasive communication techniques such as appeal to reason (logos), emotion (pathos), and credibility (ethos) to champion SDGs and audience analysis. Segmentation is also an essential rhetorical paradigm tool that can be used to tailor SDG messages and communication strategies to specific audience segments.

The Ubuntu paradigm – a new framework for communicating the SDGs

This paradigm is not a traditional PR paradigm, but it can be considered a potential PR concept in building and maintaining mutually beneficial relationships between organisations and their targeted publics from the SDG perspective. The African philosophy of Ubuntu is unique and can be translated as "a person is a person through others" or popularly paraphrased as "I am because we are, and we are because I am" (Mersham *et al.*, 2011). The centrality of this sub-Saharan African philosophy is its emphasis on humanity. It was used by the indigenous Africans in the Zulu tribe as a shared philosophy to bring people together for a common goal – to protect and value each other (Mugumbate & Nyanguru, 2013).

In the opinion of Christians (2004), African moral theory in Ubuntu philosophy is based on the communal perspective; that is, the community comes ontologically before individuals. Ubuntu's axiom "I am because we are" demonstrates a sharp contrast to the Western philosophy concept of *"cogito, ergo sum"* ("I think, therefore I am") by René Descartes. This highlights the juxtaposition between understanding human behaviour as fundamentally individual or social. Ubuntu represents a "communitarian consciousness" (Christians, 2004) and offers an alternative to individualistic liberalism. It presupposes that human identity is made through the social realm. Matolino (2020) opines that the communitarian nature of Ubuntu philosophy is exhibited through interdependence of members in the community, mutual respect and understanding, dialogue, consensus-building, inclusiveness, tolerance, transparency, and emphasis on building and nurturing relationships. These values in 'Ubuntuism', as Mersham *et al.* (2011) term it, are the lifeblood and fundamental to the public relations field.

The Ubuntu concept has been introduced into the communication and media fields by scholars such as Christians (2004), Metz (2015), Garmon & Mgijima (2012) among others. However, these scholars focused extensively on the ethical aspects of Ubuntu *vis-á-vis* communications and media. Although the Ubuntu philosophy has been popularised in the Western world, it was missing from the public relations discourse. Ngondoa & Klyueva (2023) note that despite it [Ubuntu] being a familiar concept in public relations scholarship, it has been notably missing from mainstream public relations discussions. Conversely, some African public relations scholars, like Mersham *et al.* (2011), began debating the need for an African public relations theory to build on indigenous epistemologies, particularly on the African philosophy of Ubuntu. Ubuntu-centred communication is a unique African concept with a communal worldview, meaning the community comes first, then the individual comes second.

This chapter proposes Ubuntu as a new framework for communicating the SDGs because the 17 global goals adopted by the UN in 2015 arguably entail the central principles of the Ubuntu paradigm. When SDG communication messages and strategies are designed from an Ubuntu perspective, PR practitioners can play a meaningful role in championing sustainable development and social change. The principles of Ubuntu advocate for the idea of community and collective action. This can translate into SDG PR practice of engaging with stakeholders at the grassroots level, such as the local communities, NGOs, civil society, and others. By fostering 'Ubuntuism' – inclusion and dialogue – SDG communicators can empower communities to take ownership of sustainability initiatives aligned with the SDGs. Using the Ubuntu paradigm can help build long-term and reciprocal relationships within a community and, since it places a strong emphasis on empathy, respectful dialogue, and understanding, SDG communication campaigns should involve listening to stakeholders' perspectives and concerns. Through this, communicators can build trust, foster cooperation, and mobilise collective actions in championing the 2030 Agenda and the SDGs.

Conclusion

Communicating the SDGs through public relations paradigms calls for a strategic approach leveraging various paradigms discussed in this chapter, including but not limited to Excellence and its four models, relationship management, global public relations, rhetoric, and the proposed Ubuntu concept. The Ubuntu paradigm introduced in this chapter as a potential communication paradigm for PR and the SDGs can provide a framework for designing effective SDG communication campaigns. Understanding the core principles and arguments of the paradigm is essential in implementing SDG campaigns from an Ubuntu perspective. PR plays a pivotal role in society in many aspects, including advancing the knowledge, participation, collaboration, and awareness of the SDGs.

This chapter discussed how private and state organisations can leverage the various PR paradigms to create awareness, participate, and promote the SDGs. An academically designed and tested framework must back effective communication, and the PR paradigms serve this purpose. The chapter provides a foundation for those seeking to explore the notion of PR paradigms and the SDGs regarding designing effective SDG communication campaigns based on the above-discussed PR theoretical paradigms. PR paradigms are important in shaping communication strategies and efforts to advance the SDGs. They provide diverse and rich communication frameworks to underpin SDG campaigns. Understanding the core principles and approaches advocated by the different PR paradigms, SDG communicators can develop more effective PR campaigns using one or a combination of the paradigms to engage publics, foster dialogue, and drive enthusiasm and progress towards achieving the SDGs. Each paradigm offers a unique opportunity and approach to how organisations engage with stakeholders, target publics, communicate messages, and manage relationships. All of these are relevant to promoting and advancing sustainability goals.

The chapter explored the core traditional PR paradigms in relation to designing effective communication campaigns for the SDGs. However, the various case studies examined in this book show that almost all the stakeholders engaged in the education and implementation of the SDGs used the digital approach to producing and disseminating the SDG communication activities. Future research on PR paradigms and the SDGs may focus on exploring the other modern public relations paradigms, such as the PR feminist paradigm, crisis and issue communications, corporate social responsibility, and, more particularly, the digital PR paradigms, among others. Effective communication underpinned by the PR paradigms is the lifeblood of the SDGs.

References

Akinlolu, O., Grace, B., Damilola, B. & Asekun-Olarinmoye, E. (2017). Awareness and knowledge of the Sustainable Development Goals in a university community in Southwestern Nigeria. *Ethiop J. Health Science*, 27(6), pp.669–676.

Botan, C.H., & Hazleton, V. (2006). Public Relations in a New Age. In C.H. Botan & V. Hazleton (eds.), *Public Relations Theory* II (pp.1–20). Mahwah, NJ: Lawrence Erlbaum Associates.

Brunner, B.R. (2019). What is Theory? In B.R. Brunner (ed.), *Public Relations Theory: Application and Understanding* (pp.1–12). John Wiley & Sons.

Christians, C.G. (2004). Ubuntu & communitarianism in media ethics. *Equid Novi: South African Journal for Journalism Research*, 25(2), pp.235–256.

Cutlip, S.M., Center, A.H. & Broom, G.M. (1994). *Effective Public Relations*. Prentice-Hall. https://books.google.ie/books?id=gqsbAQAAMAAJ.

Edwards, L. (2006). Public relation theories – an applied overview: Alternative approaches. *Exploring Public Relations*, pp.166–180. London: Pearsons Education.

Eurobarometer (2017). What People Know and Think About Sustainable Development. *The SDG Communicator*. https://sdg-communicator.org/data/#:~:text=Glocalities (2016) found that%2C,they knew the name only.&text=According to the latest Eurobarometer,know what the SDGs are.

Garmon, C.W. & Mgijima, M. (2012). Using Ubuntu: A New Research Trend for Developing Effective Communication acrosss Cultural Barriers. *Communication Faculty Publication*.

Grunig, J.E. (1992). What is Excellence in Management? In J.E. Grunig (ed.), *Excellence in Public Relations & Communication Management* (pp.219–250). Routledge.

Grunig, J.E. (1993). Public relations & international affairs: Effects, ethics & responsibility. *Journal of International Affairs*, 47(1), pp.137–162.

Grunig, J.E. (2008). Excellence Theory in Public Relations. In *The International Encyclopedia of Communication*. https://doi.org/10.1002/9781405186407.wbiece047.

Grunig, J.E. (2009). Paradigms of global public relations in an age of digitalisation. *PRism, 6*(2), pp.1–19. http://praxis.massey.ac.nz/prism_on-line_journ.html.

Grunig, J.E. & Grunig, L.A. (2008). Excellence Theory in Public Relations: Past, Present, & Future. In *Public Relations Research*. https://doi.org/10.1007/978-3-531-90918-9_22.

Grunig, J.E., Grunig, L.A. & Dozier, D.M. (2006). The Excellence Theory. In C.H. Botan & V. Hazleton (eds.), *Public Relations Theory II* (pp.21–62). Mahwah, NJ: Lawrence Erlbaum Associates.

Grunig, J.E., Grunig, L.A., Sriramesh, K., Huang, Y.H. & Lyra, A. (1995). Models of public relations in an international setting. *Journal of Public Relations Research*. https://doi.org/10.1207/s1532754xjprr0703_01.

Grunig, J.E. & Hunt, T. (1984). *Managing Public Relations*. Holt, Rinehart & Winston. https://books.google.ie/books?id=qCtpQgAACAAJ.

Heath, R.L. (1993). A rhetorical approach to zones of meaning and organisational prerogatives. *Public Relations Review*, 19, pp.141–155.

Heath, R.L. (2000). A rhetorical perspective on the values of public relations: Crossroads & pathways toward concurrence. *Journal of Public Relations Research*, 21(1), pp.69–91. https://doi.org/10.1207/S1532754XJPRR1201_5.

Heath, R.L. (2005). *Encyclopedia of Public Relations* (Vol. 53, Issue 9). Mahwah, NJ: Lawrence Erlbaum Associates.

Heath, R.L. & Coombs, W.T. (2006). *Today's Public Relations: An Introduction*. Thousand Oaks, CA: Sage Publications.

Kent, M.L. (2011). Public relations rhetoric: Criticism, dialogue, and the long now. *Management Communication Quarterly, 25*(3), pp.550–559. https://doi.org/10.1177/0893318911409881.

Khattab, U. (2020). Theorising Public Relations: A Historical Journey. In K. Sutherland, S. Ali & U. Khattab (eds.), *Public Relations & Strategic Communication* (pp.11–51). Oxford University Press.

L'Etang, J. (2009). Public relations and diplomacy in a globalized world: An issue of public communication. *American Behavioral Scientist, 53*(4), pp.607–626. https://doi.org/10.1177/0002764209347633.

Ledingham, J.A. (2006). Relationship Management: A General Theory of Public Relations. In C.H. Botan & V. Hazleton (eds.), *Public Relations Theory II* (pp.465–484). Mahwah, NJ: Lawrence Erlbaum Associates.

Matolino, B. (2020). Whither Epistemic Decolonization. *Philosophical Papers*, *49*(2), pp.213–231. https://doi.org/10.1080/05568641.2020.1779605.

Mersham, G., Skinner, C. & Rensburg, R. (2011). Approaches to African communication management and public relations: A case for theory-building on the continent. *Journal of Public Affairs*, *11*(4), pp.195–207. https://doi.org/10.1002/pa.413.

Metz, T. (2015). African ethics and journalism ethics: News and opinion in the light of Ubuntu. *Journal of Media Ethics*, *30*(2), pp.74–90.

Moloney, K. & McGrath, C. (2020). *Rethinking Public Relations: Persuasion, Democracy & Society*. Routledge.

Mugumbate, J. & Nyanguru, A. (2013). Exploring African philosophy: The value of Ubuntu in social work. *African Journal of Social Work*, *3*(1), pp.82–100. https://www.ajol.info/index.php/ajsw/article/view/127543/117068.

Mulholland, E. (2019). Communicating sustainable development and the SDGs in Europe: Good practice examples from policy, academia, NGOs & media. *ESDN Quarterly Reports, January 2019*, pp.1–22. https://www.sd-network.eu/quarterly reports/report files/pdf/2019-January-Communicating_Sustainable_Development_and_the_SDGs_in_Europe.pdf.

Ngondo, P.S. & Klyueva, A. (2023). Inviting an Ubuntu-Based Approach to Public Relations Theory Building in Sub-Saharan Africa. In C.H. Botan & E.J. Sommerfeldt (eds.), *Public Relations Theory III*. Routledge.

Odoom, D., Opoku, E., Christopher, M., Sagoe, D., Yiu, K., Opoku, E. & Obeng, J. (2024). Examining the level of public awareness on the Sustainable Development Goals in Africa: An empirical evidence from Ghana. *Environment, Development & Sustainability*, *26*(3), pp.6221–6238. https://doi.org/10.1007/s10668-023-02959-x.

Pfau, M. & Wan, H.-H. (2006). Persuasion: An Intrinsic Function of Public Relations. In C.H. Botan & V. Hazleton (eds.), *Public Relations Theory II* (pp.101–136). Mahwah, NJ: Lawrence Erlbaum Associates.

Pieczka, M. (2006). Paradigms, Systems Theory & Public Relations. In J.L'Etang & M. Pieczka (eds.), *Public Relations: Critical Debates & Contemporary Practice* (pp.241–269). Routledge.

Pieczka, M. (2016). Dialogue & Critical Public Relations. In J.L'Etang, D. McKie, N. Snow & J. Xifra (eds.), *The Routledge Handbook of Critical Public Relations* (pp.76–89). Routledge.

Rubtcova, M. & Pavenkov, O. (2019). Grunigian paradigm of public relations: Analysis & critics. *SSRN Electronic Journal*. https://doi.org/10.2139/ssrn.3319060.

Signitzer, B. & Prexl, A. (2007). Corporate sustainability communications: Aspects of theory & professionalization. *Journal of Public Relations Research, 20*(1), pp.1–19. https://doi.org/10.1080/10627260701726996.

Sriramesh, K. (2009). Introduction. In K. Sriramesh & D. Verčič (eds.), *The Global Public Relations Handbook, Revised & Expanded Edition: Theory, Research & Practice* (pp.xxxiii–xxxix). Routledge.

Sriramesh, K. & Verčič, D. (2009). A Theoritical Framework for Global Public Relations Research & Practice. In K. Sriramesh & D. Verčič (eds.), *The Global Public Relations Handbook, Revised & Expanded Edition: Theory, Research & Practice* (pp.3–21). Routledge.

Steyn, B. (2004). A metaphorical application of the concept 'paradigm' to the public relations domain. *Communicare, 23*(1), pp.54–78.

Taylor, M. & Kent, M.L. (2006). Public Relations Theory & Practice in Nation Building. In C.H. Botan & V. Hazleton (eds.), *Public Relations Theory II* (pp.341–374). Mahwah, NJ: Lawrence Erlbaum Associates.

Toth, E.L. & Heath, R.L. (eds.) (1992). *Rhetorical & Critical Approaches to Public Relations*. Mahwah, NJ: Lawrence Erlbaum Associates.

UNRIC (2024). Championing the SDGs: Irish organisations driving change. United Nations Regional Information Center for Western Europe. https://unric.org/en/championing-the-sdgs-irish-organisations-driving-change/.

Verwey, S. (2015). Paradigms, perspectives and practice of public relations & communication: Implications for 'Disciplined Imagination' in South African scholarship. *Communiitas*, 20, pp.1–25.

Wakefield, R.I. (1997). *International PR: A Theoretical Approach to Excellence based on a Worldwide Delphi Study*. University of Maryland.

Wang, G. (2011). Paradigm shift & the centrality of communication discipline. *International Journal of Communication, 5*, pp.1458–1466.

Yun, S.H. (2006). Toward public relations theory-based study of public diplomacy: Testing the applicability of the excellence study. *International Journal of Phytoremediation, 21*(1), pp.287–312. https://doi.org/10.1207/s1532754xjprr1804_1

Zhou, A., Capizzo, L.W., Page, T.G. & Toth, E.L. (2022). Exploring PR paradigms through computational modeling: Refractions and recommitment in public relations research (2010 - 2020) [Preprint]. *Open Science Framework, 8.5.2017*, pp.2003–2005.

V. SDG 5 – Gender Equality
WorkEqual

Molly Reilly

Abstract

The 2021 WorkEqual campaign was introduced due to the organisation's ongoing effort to achieve gender equality in Ireland. This campaign tackled ongoing issues such as the gender pay gap and caring responsibilities. Under Sonya Lennon, WorkEqual has sustained a decade-long advocacy and become a successful agent striving for real change. It strategically aligns with SDG 5 – Gender Equality, which aims to achieve gender equality for women and girls everywhere. Through various events, including the main flagship seminar, WorkEqual obtained more support from sponsorships and government bodies, spreading its important message. The campaign's success is apparent as it achieved a heightened public understanding of the issues of gender discrimination in Ireland. While facing challenges in the following years, WorkEqual has still pushed the boundaries surrounding the issue of inequality in Ireland. It serves as a continuous and vital effort to pursue a fairer Ireland and diminish the problem of gender inequality.

Introduction

Where gender equality advocacy in Ireland is concerned, one of the leading bodies is the highly successful not-for-profit organisation WorkEqual. This non-State actor advocates for women's rights and campaigns for a more equitable society. WorkEqual continues to hold yearly campaigns that have significantly changed this aspect of Irish life. The campaign being examined throughout this chapter is the 2021 WorkEqual campaign. This campaign tackled gender discrimination in Ireland with a focus on the gender pay gap issue, along with caring responsibilities, and advocating for an Ireland where policymakers and employers properly recognise family caring issues. The campaign relentlessly advocated for a society that dismantled evident barriers and tackled gender norms. The mission of WorkEqual aligns with SDG 5, a global initiative with gender equality at its centre. This SDG highlights gender equality and aims to create a fairer world for women and girls globally. It tackles various issues for women, such as inequalities in work and wages, unpaid so-called 'women's work', such as childcare and domestic work, and discrimination in public decisionmaking.

In a conversation with Sonya Lennon, founder of WorkEqual, alignment with the SDGs was not a conscious decision as WorkEqual pre-existed the invention of the SDGs. Nevertheless, aligning the organisation's values was a welcome coincidence as they saw the exact parallels. Lennon believes that "creating a society where women thrive creates a society that is better for everybody". The 2021 campaign as a case study proves the practical implementation of WorkEqual's mission. By focusing on these specific issues surrounding gender discrimination, the campaign shows the different layers of gender discrimination in Ireland.

The following section unfolds various aspects of the campaign process. First, it gives a detailed description of the background of this campaign, along with the range of achievements. The organisation's communication strategies and activities will be explored in the subsequent section, before discussing the campaign's result. A general analysis of the campaign and how it aligns with SDG 5 is also examined before concluding with lessons learnt.

Background

A decade ago, Lennon began advocating for a more equal workplace for women in Ireland, as the gender pay gap was alarmingly prevalent. Recognising the severity of the gap in Ireland, she contacted major corporations to find the root of this problem. She was met with little to no response and was constantly pushed away by organisations that refused to give her an answer. Instead of giving up, she channelled her commitment into founding WorkEqual, an organisation dedicated to advocating for women's equality in the Irish workforce. She explains that there was, and is, the issue of running an NGO in Ireland: "without funding, it can be a highly challenging environment when making real change". This pushed her to devise effective, creative ways to spread the organisation's message, beginning with WorkEqual holding annual campaigns since 2016 to tackle the reoccurring issue of gender inequality. Her mission is to "achieve full gender equality in the workplace through meaningful engagement with government, business, and civil society leaders". Its annual campaigns have garnered significant success, making profound changes for women in Ireland. Many more subsections of the public are starting to recognise gender discrepancies in other areas of Irish society.

WorkEqual has a range of goals it wants to achieve, including increasing the number of people it supports in employment each year, increasing services, and advocating for economic independence. WorkEqual believes that a better childcare system should be created so parents can fully participate in the workforce and children can avail themselves of quality early years care and education. It aims to create work bands for professional carers to help ensure a more balanced and sustainable sector, removing the burden from working men and women. The organisation also wants to create workplace incentive schemes to encourage men to share household caring duties along with optional shared parental leave for up to a year after the child's birth. Finally, it wants a legal requirement for employers to disclose their maternity and paternity leave policies. These are some of the general objectives of the WorkEqual organisation.

The 2021 campaign was a major turning point in achieving this organisational goal, and Lennon's tenacity regarding this issue has facilitated significant change for women in Ireland. This has brought the issue to the forefront for stakeholders such as the public, major corporations, and government bodies.

Tactics & Activities

The campaign held numerous events to promote its message of obtaining equality for women. First, it marked 8 November 2021 as *Equal Pay Day*, to highlight the gender pay gap in Ireland and other related issues. WorkEqual believed this was a prevalent issue in Ireland due to numerous statistics. In 2021, the gender pay gap in Ireland indicated women were paid 14.4% less than men's hourly rate. This was a significant gap, despite WorkEqual advocacy to tackle this exact statistic since 2016.

Regarding statistics surrounding caring responsibilities in Ireland, WorkEqual issued a survey to uncover public perceptions of this issue. It found that 52% of people believe that household activities such as meal planning, shopping lists, organising gifts, and social occasions are purely the job of the women in the house, with 42% believing it is equal between both the man and woman of the house, and only 2% believing it was purely the man's job. The survey also found that 48% of people believed that house chores were mainly a woman's job, while 46% believed it was a shared responsibility, and only 3% believed it was mainly a man's responsibility.

These statistics demonstrate the prevalent issue of gender inequality. The 2021 event had multiple facets to highlight the diverse issues of gender equality in Ireland. Due to Covid-19, the event was restricted, yet this did not stop WorkEqual from raising awareness. In 2021, its campaign featured a flagship online event, 'Reimagining Childcare Provision', that Roderic O'Gorman TD, Minister for Children, Equality, Disability, Integration & Youth addressed. Additionally, it unveiled market research findings that shed light on public opinion regarding gender equality. By combining the insights from the market research and the active participation of Minister O'Gorman in the event, WorkEqual effectively showcased to political decisionmakers the widespread public endorsement of government initiatives aimed at addressing gender inequalities.

This alignment, showcased during the *Equal Pay Day* event, became a powerful tool for WorkEqual to advocate for meaningful policy changes. This flagship seminar also included a range of essential guest speakers such as Frances Byrne, the director of policy and advocacy at Early Childhood Ireland, Mark Paul, the business affairs correspondent with *The Irish Times*, and finally, Sonya Lennon. They then participated in an important panel discussing addressing the issues and challenges surrounding this topic from an Irish perspective. By adapting to the changing environment of the pandemic, hosting an online event helped stretch the company's message even further. Having such a major event hosted online allowed for a broader audience to be reached, including more key policymakers.

Implementing the ideas behind the gender equality, SDG was also an important factor when pushing the WorkEqual agenda. Even if not originally intentional, the subsequent alignment with the SDGs is precise. By focusing on the campaign's different tactics through the SDGs' scope, the campaign wants to achieve the same goals.

Results & Outcomes

The 2021 campaign ended up being a huge success for WorkEqual as it created awareness of the ambition of achieving a more equitable society for women in Ireland. One of the primary results of this campaign was heightened public understanding of the issues surrounding the gender pay gap. With the help of strategic market research, it was found that over 74% of people surveyed believed that closing the gender pay cap needs to be given higher priority by employers and the government. This statistic underscores the public's growing awareness that the gender pay gap is becoming more widely acknowledged. This survey also further indicated that 70% of the respondents acknowledged that being concerned about the gender pay gap represents a genuine awareness of a significant and pressing issue. This increased concern is essential to creating a continued responsibility for garnering more support for gender equality advocacy. These findings suggest that there has been a positive and vital shift within the public, bringing more urgency to the topic.

The campaign gained more insight from the public, uncovering a range of statistics that allowed WorkEqual to understand further people's perception of gender inequality in the Irish workplace. First, when it came to workplace support for caring duties, they found a range of contrasting responses when employees were asked about workplace support. The findings are that 30% of workplaces are considered highly supportive, with people rating them between 8-10, and 24%

believing that their workplace was unsupportive, rating them lower than 5. With the rest falling in the middle, those living in middle-class areas with children in Dublin found the workplace more supportive. These findings help illuminate how major organisations treat the issues surrounding caring issues.

Another critical achievement made by the campaign was securing new sponsorships from important and successful organisations. These new sponsorships were SOLAS and permanentTSB. Securing these new headline sponsorships was a big win for the company as it now had the essential funding that could help the future advocacy activities of WorkEqual. The new funds enable WorkEqual to expand its reach and impact, conveying its message to a broader spectrum of public and private organisations. This sponsorship support helps ensure the future of the organisation and further amplifies its message of gender equality. The campaign also garnered a significant reach from all its communications outputs from 2016 to 2021, securing a reach of 63.3 million people. This was an important figure as it shows that the message of gender equality was being spread across Ireland.

Additionally, a significant achievement made by WorkEqual was being able to achieve growing participation from the Oireachtas party group. It now has a regular group of 10 parliamentarians involved, co-chaired by Ivana Bacik TD and Senators Lorraine Clifford Lee and Emer Currie. The campaign also received the support of over 47 members of the Oireachtas, and WorkEqual was mentioned 10 times in parliamentary debates. This is a massive success for the NGO as it shows that the work it has been putting in has created attraction and is starting meaningful conversations.

When looking through the scope of the SDGs, it is also apparent that it is beginning to achieve or almost has achieved some of the main sub-goals associated with gender equality. WorkEqual's first goal was to make major advances towards this campaign, which was Target 5.4. This target is to "recognise and value unpaid care and domestic work through the provision of public services, infrastructure and social protection policies and the promotion of shared responsibility within the household and the family as nationally appropriate". This was one of the campaign's main messages, and due to all the advances being made, women are becoming more recognised by the government. Yes, while significant advances have been made, it is evident there is still a lot more work to be done to address this complex issue of gender inequality in Ireland. The combination of increased public awareness, sponsorship, strategic communication, and government inclusion are all noteworthy results. Nevertheless, to continue this positive streak, the organisation needs to continue its efforts regarding equality.

Analysis

The 2021 campaign had a range of successful results, yet much work remains to be done regarding women's equality in Ireland. Since its launch in 2021, few other campaigns have had the same stretch. Lennon explains this as the organisation found it hard to garner significant sponsorships following this campaign. The 2022 and 2023 campaigns had to be severely minimised as funding was hard to obtain. However, this did not stop WorkEqual; it is now back on track with some major sponsorships coming on board in 2024, including major retailer Primark. In 2025, it will be essential for the organisation to reinforce the message of equal work. At the same time, the campaign achieved certain successes, such as garnering public support, securing major sponsorships and raising awareness. There is still a range of issues following the lack of equality for women in Ireland.

The complex nature of dismantling these deeply rooted issues is an ongoing and historical issue. WorkEqual must continue pushing for these changes to ensure Irish society becomes a more fair and equal country. The flagship online seminar was a pinnacle part of the campaign, leading to many important attractions surrounding the event. Future events could learn from the 2021 campaign by creating the same online seminar format and applying it to a physical event. This could help further push the WorkEqual's message.

Besides, including more critical figures surrounding the issue of gender discrimination could provide important insight into the organisation. With the event focused more on insights through an Irish scope, it could be highly beneficial to include the conversation in a more international scope. By inviting figures from different countries and backgrounds, WorkEqual could spread the message of gender equality to a larger audience and find new stakeholders to support them on their mission. The achievement of political inclusion was also one of the main successes of the campaign. With further inclusion from more ministers and members of the Oireachtas, WorkEqual's message could get more coverage and spread its essential message of a fairer Ireland.

Conclusion

WorkEqual has continuously tried to dismantle gender discrimination in Ireland. The organisation's ongoing campaigns since 2016 show the continued effort made to fix the issues surrounding gender discrimination. The notable successes of the 2021 campaign helped push the message of achieving gender equality regarding the gender pay gap and family caring issues. Lennon said this campaign was an enormous success overall because it "had a huge reach and helped change the national discourse in Ireland". However, to truly accomplish an equal Ireland, there needs to be a continuous concerted effort to highlight these issues.

SDG 5 wants to make an equal world for women and girls everywhere. Continued campaigns, such as the 2021 campaign by WorkEqual, will help further push the message of gender equality. Stakeholders need to support organisations such as WorkEqual by co-advocating for and putting into practice their ideas as this is an important way to achieve progress. The strategic market research done by WorkEqual helped provide important insights, uncovering the public perception surrounding the gender pay gap and caring responsibilities. This research will help educate the public on this often-hidden issue. WorkEqual also garnered support from new sponsorships such as SOLAS and permanentTSB, which will help fund further endeavours by WorkEqual. Getting the essential funding for this organisation was a crucial step in gaining more publicity as it allowed for the campaign to have a higher reach. Finally, the campaign strategically aligned with SDG 5, a crucial step in successfully achieving this goal, which will help provide a better and more equitable world for all.

Explorations

1. How effectively did WorkEqual align its messaging and tactics with SDG 5's goals of achieving gender equality and empowering women? Could it have leveraged the SDG framework more explicitly to enhance its communications and outreach efforts?

2. What additional strategies could it have used to build stronger coalitions and partnerships, amplify the campaign's impact, and drive policy change?

3. How can organisations like WorkEqual sustain momentum and secure ongoing support for their initiatives, especially in the face of financial constraints?

4. What PR strategies could be employed to maintain public interest and engagement in the long term?

5. As societal attitudes and political landscapes evolve, how should WorkEqual adapt its communications strategies to remain relevant and effective in advocating for gender equality?

VI. SDG 6 – Clean Water & Sanitation

The International Reference Centre on Community Water Supply & the WASH Programme in Ghana

Dylan Mahon

Abstract

This case study examines SDG 6, which addresses issues the clean water and sanitation sector faces and focuses on the efforts of the International Reference Centre on Community Water Supply (IRC) and the broader UN Water, Sanitation & Hygiene (WASH) initiative that they actively participate in. The study aims to fill gaps in the research and provide new insight into the goals, tactics and activities attempted thus far. The study emphasises the communication methods used from a public relations perspective, examining what has been both successful and unsuccessful for the organisation. Research methods for this case study included an interview with Marc Jaffrey, IRC's director of strategic communication. Emphasising accurate and factual sources of information, this research is critical to understanding what does and does not work from a tactical communications point of view.

Introduction

Water is necessary for many aspects of sustaining life and general health, yet the UN indicates that currently 2.2 billion people live without access to clean water for drinking and washing their hands. A further 3.5 billion lack access to safe sanitation. A consequence of this is the spread of disease throughout affected regions that could be prevented. As the global population grows, there is an increased shortage of water to meet the demand of the growing number of people occupying vulnerable regions with scarce safe water availability. Climate change itself has a significant impact, leading to water drought as temperatures increase.

Water sources that many of the world's population rely on, such as reservoirs, lakes and rivers, have been significantly affected by rising temperatures caused by global warming. Just 0.5% of water is safe and usable across the entire planet and lowering the global warming increase from 2°C to 1.5°C would decrease the population facing water scarcity by half. Diseases such as malaria, diarrhoea and cholera spread quickly through unsafe and dirty water consumption.

Clearly, access to clean water can address issues of poverty and hunger affecting those who lack it. By addressing clean water and sanitation, SDG 6 provides clear markers for improving quality of life in healthier ecosystems while sustaining economic and social advancement. While there has been considerable progress over the last two decades, SDG 6 aims to address most of the issues by 2030 and there is still much to do to ensure this timeline is met. Critical to addressing these issues by 2030 is a target to develop sustainable infrastructure with long-term benefits such as maintaining management of wastewater, and resources and preserving ecosystems for locally affected populations.

Background

The organisation this case study focuses on is the International Reference Centre on Community Water Supply (IRC) and specifically its involvement with WASH. IRC, a non-profit organisation operating in many different regions across the world, was founded in 1968 as a joint effort between the government of the Netherlands and the World Health Organization (WHO). IRC aims to achieve the primary target of bringing access and long-term sustainability to the areas where it works, bringing access to clean water and ongoing sustainability to at least a further 1 million people by 2030. Thus far, its campaign has successfully reached over 3.6 million people globally and, through its collaboration with Water for People, looks to directly impact 20 million. It also aims to maintain its advocacy for over 200 million people globally. The organisation is actively working with governments and country leaders to achieve their goals.

Through the WASH initiative, IRC wants to support governments in six countries in South Asia and sub-Saharan Africa. The initiative aims to lead to better health and increased equality outcomes in the countries where it operates. The WASH system was designed to take a human approach and to use the involvement of people at a global and national level. It looks at environmental, financial and infrastructure elements and takes a philosophical systems approach that aims to create a new way of thinking about issues for long-term progress and development in the sector that are pragmatically and realistically sustainable.

There should be a significant increase in financial support in affected areas looking to achieve the WASH targets. Governments currently lack the financial resources to successfully implement recommendations. Currently, the finances require over $1.7 trillion globally, which is far beyond the finances available currently. Several countries involved in the WASH sector require an increase over six times their current levels of spending. In countries involved with the WASH sector, over 40% do not have plans to consistently finance sustainable systems. Governments also face fiscal difficulties as well, thus preventing them from allocating the funds successfully to reach goals at a national level.

There has been significant progress made in the WASH sector in the last two decades. The approach has evolved along with the campaign. The main issue is grappling with the necessity for people to pay for these services, along with understanding the financial implications for each region and their ability to access the funds necessary to sustain them. There needs to be an emphasis on working with economists who understand the sector's requirements and how to allocate finances correctly. Frameworks need to be considered that provide the correct incentives for those with scarce resources to leverage them and use other inputs they have efficiently.

Figures from WHO reveal that the current trajectory for achieving SDG 6 is off by a factor of four, meaning that the current numbers evaluating success are four times smaller than projected. This indicates that SDG 6 is currently destined to fail. This is consistent with information and data gathered by the UN. It places an imperative on those currently campaigning – from SWA, the intergovernmental agency for SDG 6, to IRC as a disruptive thought leader – to encourage some of the larger players involved to act and impose an obligation to think radically differently about what needs to be done. This new thinking is not geared toward achieving SDG 6 by 2030, as that is currently unrealistic, but to reset course. SDG 6 does not ask for everyone to have safe water like those in developed countries: it aims to ensure basic access. This can include walking up to 300 meters for some level of safe water access.

Tactics & Activities

Between 2017 and 2021, IRC Ghana collaborated with the government of Ghana in a strategic plan to achieve progress in the country relating to issues of the WASH initiative and reaching the goals of SDG 6 and the government. The government created an SDG coordination desk and developed a new ministry: the Ministry of Sanitation & Water Resources. This ministry had the aim of implementing an effective strategy for delivering improved water and sanitation services in the country. This was done with the government's intent to develop a strategic plan for tackling the issues of the sector. They found that, although

Ghana did meet the drinking water target, they did not meet the target of overall improved sanitation. Compared to drinking water, basic access to sanitation and waste management services was extremely limited, with a substantial amount of the population lacking bathroom facilities. Over half of the country's population lacked access to proper hygiene training and handwashing facilities. Although Ghana typically has an abundance of freshwater resources, this can change significantly depending on time of year and factors such as climate change. Ghana's water supply also faces the issue of meeting demands of a growing population, leading to increased pollution and conflict relating to water resources. The responsibilities of the ministry include overseeing companies involved with delivering the services, educating the public on hygiene, managing resources, and protecting the environment.

The issue was quite technical: to build into the risk and financial systems the ability to integrate climate risk and projections on costs, infrastructure and development. While this was understandable to professional audiences, it did not translate into anything understandable for local communities and activist groups. Strategic communications must be done correctly and appropriately tailored to each targeted group. Ghanaian communities are largely aware that their lives are vulnerable in multiple ways, not least of which is climate, which brings another level of vulnerability. In quite simple terms, they are aware that there is a water crisis and that it is linked to the climate crisis. They do not need to be informed further to develop awareness of the issue's existence. However, a more considered, strategic approach is needed to assert this is not just an issue of too much or too little water: there needs to be robust and resilient systems to manage the water supply. To achieve this, there should be a much more powerful citizen voice programme, just as in the past, there were programmes that pre-dated social media, such as video diary programmes around gathering citizen voices that could be harvested.

The publics for the IRC's WASH initiatives are government officials, districts, mayors, government agencies and various teams specialising in water and sustainability. Building strong relationships in the target regions is especially important as collaboration is vital for both short- and long-term success. Getting educators, teachers, and schools on board is also a priority when it comes to educating the population on good hygiene practices. Using communication tactics depends on who the audience is from a policy and development point of view. There should be an emphasis on climate change awareness when looking at the many districts with whom IRC has worked over long periods of time in order to support mayors, chief executives, and teams across different disciplines in working on water issues.

One high-level communication tactic IRC Ghana has taken is to work with the Coalition of NGOs in Water & Sanitation (CONIWAS), an umbrella civil society organisation in Ghana. This is an excellent example of coalition building with a like-minded organisation in practice. The collaboration aims to increase education and advocacy efforts to minimise the limitations of poverty and achieve the goals of WASH in non-urban areas of the country. The organisation will also collaborate with Ghana Water Company Limited to achieve its mandate of providing safe water access to every urban community currently without access.

A sub-campaign of IRC within the WASH sector was Voices for Water. Organised by the Watershed project, of which the IRC is a member organisation, the main purpose of the campaign was to sustain interest in the water issue as, according to Marc Jaffrey, the overall project design was at fault: it was an example of a technical sector that lacked knowledge about who they were trying to influence or how to influence them successfully. It was unclear what the campaign was attempting to disrupt and did not really have anything to encourage the Ghanaian government to act. This points to the difficulties posed by implementing top-down solutions without considering how best to communicate them to critical publics and offers evidence that strategic communications must be built into campaigns. Refocused, Voices for Water connected at a personal level, with testimonials from individuals forming part of the lobbying and advocacy. It focused on four simple steps that encouraged individuals and government agencies: find the evidence, follow the money, secure their water and be part of the process. It transformed the communication process from one-way and technocratic to participatory, community-level engagement.

Toilet Talks, another sub-campaign of the IRC and WASH sector aimed to create a wider interest in people who might be involved with other types of social policies. Hosted by Ikenna Azuike, an award-winning journalist and filmmaker, it launched with five broadcast episodes in which he interviewed people about important social issues. Both Azuike and his guests, including the Ghanaian environmental activist, Chibeze Ezekiel, were seated on their toilets for the duration of the interviews. What made the broadcasts so interesting from a strategic communications perspective is that they were intersectional, connecting water and sanitation to broader social justice issues, including health, education, gender and economic development. Having a diverse body of social activists participating in soft social discourse was effective. IRC found that it acted as a bridge, particularly for younger people whose interest was ignited by the human rights aspect of it. There was a sense that new audiences were being reached by the campaign.

Although the issue of water security has not been resolved and continues to be one of global importance, the outcomes IRC achieved were a result of encouraging the technical water sector to think that its work could be made interesting and more discursive. IRC centred its campaigns around the human story, and attempted to include more people who were not already talking about water or were only tangential to a larger discourse. This approach is part of a suite of work that IRC is trying to build at an informal, soft level for activists and communities. The soft approach encourages the idea that water and sanitation communications is not just for governments, professionalised NGOs and organisations with a technical focus. For Jaffrey, this approach comes from a theory of change, and the understanding that says public health indicators in a country will not improve unless every level from the bottom up, from communities to water engineers, to government agencies to ministries addresses the issue.

Results & Outcomes

Ghana has made considerable progress by allying strategic communications to the water campaigns. Education and public awareness have helped the country move closer to achieving the goal of improving sustainable water solutions. There has been a significant increase in stakeholder knowledge and participation because of the WASH systems campaign. There is a deeper understanding of the services required to achieve SDG 6-related goals and services. Throughout the duration of WASH thus far, stakeholders have increasingly conceptualised effective ideas. The approach has proved successful, increasing awareness of involved stakeholders to be more proactive.

Since beginning its journey in Ghana, the IRC has moved closer to achieving the goal of improving sustainable water solutions. IRC collaborated with the National Development Planning Commission (NDPC), a Ghanaian state agency, which agreed to keep a record of good sector practice within areas of the country and publish their findings. IRC Ghana also created a strategy plan for the period 2022 and 2026. The government's mission is now to achieve the goals of SDG 6 across Ghana by 2030, aligning with the overall aim of SDG 6 laid out by the UN. In 2021, they developed a WASH toolkit with the support of IRC. The toolkit has been verified and is set to be used during the 2022–2026 strategic plan, and the findings will be used to learn how to improve WASH planning in the future. IRC Ghana has strengthened relationships with ministries in the sector and other agencies. The organisation is going to broaden the sanitation programme and create new strategies in collaboration with WASH and different sectors. It will continue to strengthen and develop new relationships with the private sector to expand the delivery of WASH services and improve existing services. Some intermediate outcomes that IRC Ghana have considered as a good measurement of success towards achieving SDG 6 include increased political will to act at the top level, key players able to improve service throughout the country, and planning and regulation. Citizens demanding improved services for a better quality of life point to the effectiveness of public campaigns like Voices for Water and Toilet Talks.

Critical Analysis

SDG 6 is a complex issue with many elements that make it difficult to achieve successfully. The reliance on human empathy and involvement can make it difficult to achieve the delivery of even basic systems. Communication should be two-way. The idea of getting citizens involved through various sub-campaigns seems to be the correct approach to take; however, it requires active participants on both ends. Working closely with districts and ministries is a good start, although it hinges on the ability of the government, districts, ministries, and NGOs within the country to communicate clearly with the local and national population to deliver the message of working towards a goal that is beneficial to everyone in the country and will significantly increase their quality of life. Education initiatives are worthwhile, but only if they are consistent across the entire country. The earlier education on hygiene is taught in schools, the better the long-term outcome of achieving the goals of SDG 6.

To achieve measurable success by organisations such as IRC, continued communication with governments, ministries and districts is vital. It has proven to have measurable success in Ghana; however, the ongoing communication plan between 2022 and 2026 indicates that progress has been slower since the 2017-2021 plan was implemented. It could be a fruitful endeavour to engage with the same ministries, districts and NGOs, in a manner that leads to the success in parts of the country currently lacking the necessary services, encouraging goals across the nation in a unitive effort between the ministries and districts currently participating. The knowledge from training and education gained thus far by ministries and district could be used to communicate with other districts in the underserviced parts of the country for more definitive and ongoing success if co-operation is achieved.

Conclusion

Water is necessary for sustaining life and preventing disease and issues that arise from lacking basic access to it. It can be argued that, among the Sustainable Development Goals, SDG 6 is one of, if not the, most vital to achieve at this moment in time. Climate change affects the entire planet; however, it is having catastrophic consequences in regions where access to clean, safe water is scarce. It should be tackled on a global level for meaningful improvement. Although funds are being generated consistently, $1.7 trillion is a mammoth task with regards to generating sufficient funding. This is a difficult reality for the regions that require the most intervention from global organisations trying to implement change when they already struggle significantly from an economic standpoint.

SDG 6 is unlikely to be achieved by 2030; however, that does not indicate that considerable progress towards it cannot be achieved by then. It requires consistent communication between organisations, citizens and those in positions of power to institute change in a manner that leads to long-term sustainability as opposed to short-term solutions. Education is a necessity, as well as community and public participation, and should continue to be emphasised in the future. The issues that SDG 6 address will continue to affect countries without basic, safe access to clean water for many years to come. If the burden on affected regions can be lightened, even slightly, then quality of life could be improved significantly. IRC's approach of working with districts, ministries, NGOs and government agencies in Ghana has led to respectable, but moderate, success. If it can capitalise on the relationships it has developed, and continue with targeted communications campaigns, progress can continue, and Ghana can benefit from the education initiatives to maximise the water resources it has.

Explorations

1. This campaign found that the technical language of water experts was not understood by the ordinary citizen. Assess the challenges of rephrasing technical language into easily understandable messages for mass audiences.

2. What additional strategies could the IRC have used to build stronger coalitions and partnerships?

3. Human stories were a feature of this campaign. How might the IRC use creative storytelling techniques to build on the successes already achieved?

4. How might Constance Chay-Nemeth's work on publics help identify new strategies for communicating with audiences?

5. Many campaigns in the developing world have origins in Western thinking. How might the philosophy of Ubuntu have made this campaign more meaningful for ordinary Ghanaians?

VII. SDG 7 – Affordable & Clean Energy
UCC's Tyndall Institute Kiln Building

Seán Ivory

Abstract

Tyndall National Institute and the Sustainable Energy Authority of Ireland (SEAI) have partnered to launch a campaign highlighting Tyndall's newly renovated energy-efficient facility, which was made possible by implementing ISO 50001. This international standard provides a structured framework for organisations to optimise their energy consumption, outlining steps to establish, maintain, and enhance energy management systems. The ISO framework will work with the Excellence in Energy Efficiency Design (EXEED) process to maximise efficiency. This collaborative campaign also aims to raise awareness of Sustainable Development Goal (SDG) 7, focusing on affordable and clean energy. It showcases the tangible impact of SDG 7 on University College Cork's community, offering innovative solutions that can be adopted in future projects. The initiative demonstrates the power of collaboration in achieving sustainable goals and inspires others to act toward a cleaner energy future.

Introduction

Tyndall National Institute is at the forefront of combating the pollution caused by fossil fuels, prioritising the transition to renewable energy sources. This initiative aligns with SDG 7, which aims to ensure access to affordable, reliable, sustainable, and modern energy for all. This goal is part of a broader framework of 17 SDGs established by the UN in 2015, intended to guide global development efforts across 102 countries.

SDG 7 is of particular significance due to the fact that 675 million individuals, predominantly in sub-Saharan Africa, remain without access to electricity. This urgency is heightened by the annual decrease in international funding for clean energy projects in developing regions. Although modern renewables account for almost 30% of the world's electricity, their contribution to heating and transport still needs to be improved, highlighting the need for continued innovation and investment.

Despite these challenges, a global movement towards achieving the UN's 2030 targets is gaining momentum. Nations such as Ireland are collaborating with developing countries to foster a healthier planet, illustrating the power of international cooperation in addressing complex environmental issues. The primary objectives of SDG 7 encompass enhancing energy efficiency, advancing cleaner and renewable energy technologies, establishing financial mechanisms to achieve energy security and environmental sustainability, promoting further research and development, and generating employment in this sector.

Tyndall and the UN are committed to moving away from destructive fossil fuels and embracing modern technology that allows for sustainable energy solutions, which will have both financial benefits and help the transition towards a cleaner, greener environment. Tyndall's project aligns with several targets outlined by the UN, including increasing the share of renewable energy and accelerating improvements in energy efficiency. Target 7a is particularly relevant, as it emphasises the importance of cooperation between organisations and public relations firms to raise awareness of decarbonisation efforts and promote clean energy research and technology. Substantial investment in energy infrastructure and research is crucial to combat the reliance on fossil fuels and achieve cleaner air and environments. This investment will drive the development and adoption of renewable energy solutions and foster a healthier planet for future generations. By focusing on these critical areas, Tyndall and its partners actively contribute to a sustainable energy future by focusing on these critical areas.

Since the introduction of the 17 SDGs, progress towards SDG 7 has been a mixed bag of successes and setbacks. On a positive note, the global population with access to electricity increased from 87% in 2015 to 91% in 2021, and the share of renewable energies in the global energy mix grew from 16.7% to 19.1% during the same period. However, this progress has been hampered by a notable decline in international financial support for clean energy in developing countries, particularly before and during the Covid-19 pandemic. This decline is alarming, with 2021 figures showing $10.8 billion in support, less than half of the $26.4 billion invested in 2017, signalling a need for a renewed commitment to sustainable energy funding in these regions.

Background

Tyndall National Institute, a leading Irish research centre in integrated information and communications technology, is an integral part of University College Cork. With over 600 members in its multidisciplinary research community, Tyndall specialises in electronics and photonics. Its current project, focused on decarbonisation and energy efficiency, aligns with the Irish government's 2030 decarbonisation campaign. This ambitious initiative, scheduled for completion in mid-2025, exemplifies Tyndall's commitment to a sustainable future.

A vital aspect of this project involves upgrading the historic Kiln building, initially constructed in 1903. The challenge was transforming this century-old structure into a modern research facility while prioritising sustainable, affordable, and reliable energy solutions. By implementing demand control measures for lighting, heating, ventilation, and power, Tyndall aims to maintain quality while simultaneously reducing energy consumption and costs. This approach benefits the environment and allows the Institute to redirect financial resources towards other renewable energy initiatives and research projects. The Kiln building's transformation serves as an exemplary model of how historic structures can be adapted to meet the demands of the 21st century while embracing sustainability.

Collaborating with the SEAI offers Tyndall National Institute a wealth of benefits, drawing on SEAI's track record of successful campaigns with numerous organisations dedicated to decarbonisation, energy efficiency, and renewable energy. Tyndall recognises the immense value of the publicity generated through this partnership, which promotes University College Cork and reinforces the core values of wellness and sustainability championed by both organisations. This collaboration builds upon a longstanding relationship between Tyndall and SEAI, spanning almost two decades, and fosters a deep understanding of shared goals. Furthermore, Tyndall maintains a constant dialogue with clients, governing bodies, and funding agencies like the European Investment Bank, all working towards common objectives in sustainability and energy efficiency. This open communication and forging new relationships with clients and investors naturally generate positive word-of-mouth, bolstering Tyndall's reputation and fostering greater engagement with its mission.

From the project's outset, Tyndall set ambitious goals for this project in its strategic plan. The vision included achieving a remarkable 51% carbon reduction by 2030 compared to a 2016-2018 baseline. In the near term, Tyndall aimed for 2% savings on 2021's total final consumption and focused on project development to accelerate decarbonisation in 2022. Senior leadership regularly reviewed progress to ensure these objectives remained on track and aligned with Tyndall's overall strategy. The energy programme and action plans were continuously updated, complemented by annual independent audits. This meticulous approach reflects Tyndall's unwavering commitment to achieving its sustainability targets and leading energy efficiency.

Tyndall's adoption of SEAI's Excellence in Energy Efficiency Design (EXEED) process proved instrumental in understanding the Kiln building's energy consumption patterns, identifying improvements, and quantifying potential savings. This comprehensive analysis paved the way for a strategic plan to drive Tyndall's decarbonisation efforts. The trust between Tyndall and SEAI, solidified by Tyndall's impressive record of accomplishment of eight SEAI Energy Awards over the past two decades, ensured a seamless collaboration from both energy efficiency and public relations perspectives. This strong foundation set the stage for a successful partnership and a powerful demonstration of Tyndall's commitment to sustainability.

Tactics & Activities

Tyndall National Institute approached its energy-efficient design project with a meticulous strategic plan, aiming to achieve positive environmental outcomes and widespread recognition for its efforts. Professor William Scanlon, CEO of Tyndall, emphasised the Institute's dedication to tackling sustainability challenges like climate change, energy conservation, and water management. These research endeavours have significantly elevated the Institute's national and international profile.

The implementation in 2012 of ISO 50001, an international standard that helps organisations to continually reduce energy use, lower energy costs and greenhouse gas emissions, has been a cornerstone of Tyndall's remarkable progress toward its ambitious goals of a 50% improvement in energy efficiency and a 51% reduction in CO_2 emissions. This standard provided a structured framework for its energy management system, ensuring continuous investment in energy performance improvement activities. Senior management plays a crucial role in maintaining this system and fostering collaboration among stakeholders within the institute. Cormac Harrington, the Chief Operations Officer, oversees objectives, targets, and action plans, ensuring their effectiveness through regular meetings and management reviews. This meticulous internal communications approach reflects Tyndall's unwavering commitment to achieving its sustainability targets and leading the way in energy efficiency.

To further enhance its understanding of the Kiln building's energy consumption and unlock even more significant savings, Tyndall embraced SEAI's EXEED process alongside ISO 50001. This strategic move allowed it to expand its long-term decarbonisation strategy and explore innovative solutions. The EXEED process proved invaluable, revealing 123 potential improvements focused on reducing energy demand through operational control and optimisation. In the second phase, Tyndall prioritised energy projects, beginning with operational control enhancements, followed by low / medium cost demand reduction projects, and finally, capital-intensive decarbonisation initiatives. As a culmination of their efforts, heat pumps were installed for efficient heating and cooling once the energy demand had been significantly reduced. This systematic approach showcases Tyndall's unwavering commitment to maximising energy efficiency and minimising its carbon footprint.

Achieving carbon neutrality is a top priority for Tyndall National Institute. Its strategic plan outlines ambitious annual objectives and targets, reviewed by senior leadership to ensure progress towards this goal. Regular internal conferences, management meetings, and energy reviews keep Tyndall focused on meeting the requirements of funding agencies and governing bodies, while collaborating effectively with SEAI to promote their vital campaign. Several key steps are taken to measure the project's success and maintain high standards. These include presenting objectives, targets, and action plans to secure financial and other resources. Monthly energy team meetings facilitate the review of energy performance indicators and project status, ensuring ongoing progress and accountability.

The partnership between Tyndall and SEAI extends beyond the EXEED process, with SEAI playing a crucial role in this campaign's public relations and communications aspects. Recognising such projects is paramount to Tyndall, the Irish government, and the UN, as it helps raise awareness and engagement among target audiences regarding SDG 7 and the importance of energy efficiency and renewable energy. Increased support for these initiatives can lead to more significant funding for innovative projects, propelling progress towards the UN's ambitious targets. While the full impact of this ongoing project, set to continue until October 2024, has yet to be fully assessed, the initial results are promising. The collaboration between Tyndall and SEAI demonstrates the power of combining technical expertise with effective communication to drive positive change and inspire a sustainable future.

Results & Outcomes

Tyndall is transparent in the projects it undertakes and the subsequent results from a strategic communications and media perspective and is attempting to get closer to its long-term decarbonisation goal. Apart from the unforeseen circumstances of Covid-19 in 2020, the Institute is making significant progress towards its energy efficiency targets. This transparency is critical for reflecting progress towards achieving their energy efficiency targets and raising awareness of their initiatives, fostering trust and engagement among stakeholders. The importance of tracking and reporting these results cannot be overstated. Projects like ISO 50001 certification and the awards received during the initiative are presented in annual reports and published on Tyndall's website, ensuring accountability and public recognition of their efforts.

Reflecting on the project's results, Tyndall pinpoints three critical areas for future improvement:

- First, interdepartmental communication is crucial for data collection and reporting about performance issues and upgrades. Enhancing communication channels ensures collaboration, efficiency and transparency that will ensure smoother project planning and feature implementation, minimising disruptions for staff;
- Second, providing early and comprehensive training in energy-efficient design, procurement and the benefits of the system to all staff is crucial. As Tyndall grows, embedding the company's core values of sustainability into every aspect of work, from systems to procedures, becomes paramount: proper training empowers staff to contribute effectively to energy efficiency initiatives, maximising the project's impact, and achieving the strategic communications goals through demonstrated, measurable activity. All future projects must be carbon neutral-ready from the outset, aligning with Tyndall's ambitious decarbonisation goals;
- Finally, more robust controls on building management and data collection systems are necessary. Due to increased usage, the integrity of operational controls and energy metering data has eroded over time. Tightening these controls will ensure accurate and reliable data, crucial for informed decisionmaking, and for formulating internal communications.

The valuable lessons gained from this project pave the way for even greater success in Tyndall's future endeavours. The Institute's commitment to continuous improvement and its focus on sustainability promise a bright and impactful future. The circumstances during the Covid-19 pandemic make the success of the campaign even more impressive due to having design team meetings *via* Zoom, as well as material shortages and cost inflation, being the two key issues to overcome. The recognition of this project is showcased with the granting of the Energy in Buildings Award at the SEAI's 2021 awards. The organisation has achieved the third highest building energy rating of A3. This project exemplifies how other buildings of this age and structure must be improved to reach contemporary carbon standards.

Tyndall enjoys strong support from top government figures like the then Taoiseach, Cork-based Micheál Martin, and Tánaiste, though this backing is for both the Institute and its specific projects and campaigns. Raising awareness of Tyndall's efforts, showcasing its clients' achievements, and highlighting the importance of SDG 7 are crucial to leveraging this high-level support for maximum impact. It highlights the need for Tyndall's marketing and communications team to promote this campaign strategically. Tyndall emphasises the crucial role of the media and relevant organisations in making energy information relatable to everyday citizens, and not something abstract or complicated. It uses channels, media, coalition-building and social media, including Twitter / X, Instagram, and LinkedIn to further the communications goal of bridging the gap between individual energy consumption in households and the massive scale of research facilities like Tyndall. Furthermore, projects like Tyndall's innovative energy efficiency design can be powerful inspirations for the next generation. These initiatives can ignite a passion for working in the industry and drive a collective push towards a healthier environment. Ultimately, the accurate measure of success for Tyndall's strategic plan lies in a combination of tangible project results and the positive media attention it garners. This dual approach showcases the institute's concrete achievements and amplifies its message and impact on a broader scale.

Critical Analysis

The project's success is underscored by several significant achievements, including offsetting 723 tons of carbon dioxide emissions, achieving a 29% reduction in energy consumption, and generating annual savings of approximately €329,817. Moreover, the broader team at Tyndall, including facilities and operations personnel, was fully engaged, and there was a desire to continue to EXEED stage 2 due to energy, cost, and carbon savings. While Tyndall and the SEAI have made strides in their communications efforts, there must be more focus on broadening the campaign's reach. Engaging with prominent media outlets and publications focused on sustainability or emerging technologies could significantly amplify their message. Although political figures like the Taoiseach and Tánaiste have visited Tyndall, their presence has not explicitly been tied to this campaign, and securing the endorsement of high-profile political figures would be invaluable in raising the campaign profile to ignite public interest and spark greater engagement with the campaign while highlighting the UN's SDGs and Tyndall's innovative projects.

Social media is critical for organisations seeking to spread their message. Tyndall actively leverages social media platforms like Twitter / X, Instagram, and LinkedIn to disseminate key messages and information about the campaign and energy-efficient initiatives. However, a more targeted and strategic social media approach tailored to this campaign could further elevate its visibility and impact. Additionally, adding regular project updates *via* YouTube consistently or on any of its current social channels would have benefited greatly in showing the process behind the project. Broader media engagement, highlighting the successes, challenges and people involved in its implementation would allow for more connectivity and engagement from Tyndall's clients and those looking to take inspiration from it. Furthermore, endorsements from those who use the research facility, UCC students, and outside sustainability management experts could help gain even more credibility. Expanding media coverage beyond Tyndall's immediate circle of influence is essential to reach a broader audience and inspire more significant action towards achieving SDG 7. Nonetheless, Tyndall has made some positive decisions regarding those in leadership positions. It has effectively used leading figures in the company, such as Derry Kelleher and Tim Cronin, to explain the process and benefits of the campaign as well as how Tyndall wants to progress in the future. Tyndall's plans include a strategic plan, 'Tyndall 2025', aiming to double the size of the Institute and to secure a global leadership position for Ireland in deep-tech research.

Conclusion

The work of Tyndall National Institute exemplifies how an organisation can make a meaningful contribution to achieving the global targets set by the UN and the Irish government regarding renewable, sustainable energy. The Kiln building project showcases a successful approach to energy efficiency, decarbonisation, and sustainability. Tyndall's transparent reporting, continuous improvement efforts, and strategic collaboration with SEAI underscore its dedication to achieving SDG 7 targets and promoting energy efficiency. Nonetheless, although there are no communications crises or negative media coverage of this campaign, and although Tyndall's strategic plans and efforts have garnered recognition and support within its immediate network, more substantial coverage from media outlets apart from the SEAI's own channels could have been achieved. Broader media engagement and high-profile endorsements could significantly amplify its impact and inspire more substantial public and institutional involvement. The SEAI is an influential organisation; however, analysis and praise from other publications and institutions not directly linked to Tyndall could help give it more organic credibility and support from different funding agencies and clients. There is room for growth due to the relevance of SDG 7 and the constant discussions in the media surrounding climate change, sustainability and the environment, and other audiences can be found. Awareness and campaigns from younger generations are only expanding in size, and social media being the contemporary tool for communications and assisting in achieving the targets for SDG 7. By building on their successes and expanding their outreach efforts, Tyndall can play a pivotal role in driving global progress towards a cleaner, greener, and more sustainable future.

Explorations

1. Evaluate Tyndall's media relations efforts during the campaign. Did it effectively use traditional and digital media to raise awareness about the project and its connection to SDG7?

2. How could Tyndall have used its strategic relationship with high-profile figures national politicians to amplify its message?

3. How could Tyndall and the SEAI develop a more comprehensive PR strategy to raise broader public awareness of their energy efficiency initiatives, aligning with SDG 7's objectives?

4. How could Tyndall leverage this project to position itself as leaders in decarbonisation and renewable energy? What PR strategies could it implement to maintain and enhance its reputation in this area?

5. The partnership between Tyndall and SEAI was crucial. How could similar partnerships between research institutions, government agencies and NGOs be developed in other communications campaigns to promote sustainable development for broader societal impact?

VIII. Intermezzo 2
Public Relations Theory & Its Evolving Role in Communication with Publics
Cliodhna Pierce

The SDGs: A Public Engagement Imperative for Sustainable Development

The UN SDGs offer a comprehensive roadmap for achieving a sustainable future that addresses interconnected social, economic, and environmental challenges. As Deacon (2016) noted, the SDGs represent a significant milestone in global policy, outlining a vision for international collaboration. While the SDGs provide a valuable framework for policymakers and stakeholders, their success ultimately hinges on widespread public support and participation. To achieve buy-in, long-lasting communication strategies must move beyond mere awareness campaigns and actively foster dialogue with diverse audiences. Understanding how the public conceptualises the SDGs and sustainability more broadly is essential for developing messages that resonate, ultimately leading to a greater uptake of sustainable practices and increased pressure on authorities to prioritise sustainability initiatives. (Bain *et al.*, 2019).

Effectively implementing the SDGs necessitates a multifaceted approach transcending mere policy formulation and corporate sustainability pledges. It demands a strategic communication strategy that engages the public, transforming them from passive information recipients into empowered participants and problem-solvers. By fostering a comprehensive understanding of public perceptions, tailoring messages to resonate with diverse viewpoints, and nurturing inclusive dialogue, we can unlock the transformative potential inherent in the SDGs. Information that resonates with an individual's value systems and worldview is perceived as more credible and engaging. This, in turn, fosters greater information sharing and amplification through social networks. Consequently, effective sustainability communication hinges on understanding prevailing public perceptions of the SDGs. This chapter will probe into the insights gleaned from the case studies in this book, dissecting and discussing them within the framework of the four most referenced theories of public, systems theory, situational theory, Chay-Nemeth's theory, Grunig's four models, and linkage theory.

Reconceptualising Public Engagement for Sustainable Development Communication

Prioritising publics is one of the most essential components of public relations practice. The concept of publics in the context of PR has advanced significantly over time (Grunig, 1997). Initially rooted in early models of mass communication, the term 'general public' emerged as a broad, standardised category encompassing all members of society who were potential recipients of communication messages. This simplistic view of audiences as passive receivers prevailed during the early stages of PR practice, reflecting a one-way communication model in which organisations disseminated messages to a mass audience without considering individual differences or preferences.

This section of case studies highlights the critical role of public understanding in unlocking the true potential of the SDGs. A stakeholder priority hierarchy emerges by synthesising the Grunig & Hunt (1984) linkage model with the Mitchell *et al.* (1997) salience model. Engaging with diverse stakeholders, from investors and regulators to community activists, who wield significant influence, is crucial for long-term success. Strategic communication fosters understanding and empowers these stakeholders, creating a collaborative environment where everyone's interests are aligned. The framework presented here builds upon the foundations Chay-Nemeth (2001) and Grunig (2000) laid to establish a more nuanced approach to public engagement within SDGs. Schram (1954) emphasised that successful communication hinges on the communicator's understanding of the audience's frame of reference. Similarly, Chay-Nemeth (2001) advocated for comprehending stakeholders' specific interests and concerns and the power relations that influence that dynamic.

Public support is vital for the broader adoption of sustainable technologies and programmes and to hold authorities and businesses accountable. Heath's (1998) exploration of the public sphere in the new media age highlighted the potential for previously passive publics to become active participants. This necessitates a shift in how we conceptualise publics, moving beyond sender-receiver models towards a more dynamic view. These frameworks offer a multi-pronged approach to public engagement for SDG communication, drawing on stakeholder theory from Chay-Nemeth (2001) and the Grunig model (2000).

This combined approach offers multifaceted benefits by integrating targeted communication with stakeholder engagement. Well-crafted messages tailored to specific publics and their interests effectively promote understanding and action. This approach can cultivate collaborative solutions alongside public engagement by fostering a dialogue that connects crucial stakeholders. This two-way process fosters a richer pool of ideas and a stronger sense of collective ownership over sustainability initiatives. By addressing stakeholders' diverse needs and perspectives, such communication strategies contribute to achieving the SDGs sustainably over time. However, the external landscape and public priorities constantly evolve; therefore, this framework should be flexible and adaptable to accommodate such dynamic changes. Finding common ground and fostering collaboration amidst diverse perspectives requires carefully applying communication strategies. The case studies presented in this book further underscore the urgency of promoting public engagement in sustainability initiatives.

Publics as Dynamic Partners: A Systems Theory Perspective on Communicating SDGs

Ludwig von Bertalanffy's mid-20th-century systems theory challenged organisations' perceptions of being isolated entities. Instead, systems theory proposes that organisations are open systems engaged in constant exchange with their environment. Publics are integral to this environment, shaped by organisational actions and communication. Organisations can foster transparency and build meaningful relationships by identifying relevant publics, their concerns, and appropriate levels of engagement. PR thrives on understanding the dynamic relationships between organisations and their public, and systems theory offers a powerful analytical lens for understanding organisational complexity. This perspective emphasises the nature of organisations as open systems, deeply influenced by and influencing a complex, interconnected external environment. The interdependence of organisations and various publics is emphasised, highlighting how changes in one element impact the entire system. Publics, alongside employees and competitors, are crucial to the organisational ecosystem. Thus, effective communication is vital for maintaining this equilibrium and achieving SDGs.

Effective communication hinges on recognising the heterogeneity of publics, and segmentation based on shared interests is crucial for tailoring communication strategies that strengthen relationships with these diverse groups (Grunig, 1997). James Grunig's (1997) distinction between stakeholders and publics clarifies this vital nuance. While organisations can choose stakeholders, the public emerges organically from shared issues and concerns (Dewey, in Grunig, 1997). Livesey (2001) emphasised the importance of language and symbolic action in establishing a symmetrical dialogue with these diverse publics. This interdependence between organisations and their publics forms the cornerstone of effective communication. Organisations rely on the public for resources, legitimacy, and support, while publics are simultaneously influenced by organisational actions and communication (Grunig, 1997). It is a dynamic that necessitates a two-way communication process, which can only be effectively implemented within an open system framework. Such a framework allows organisations to actively listen to public concerns and adapt their messaging strategies accordingly. From a systems theory perspective, the public can be conceptualised as subsystems within the broader organisational environment, exerting influence on and being influenced by the organisation (Rosenau, 1984).

Within an open systems framework, effective SDG communication necessitates listening to public concerns and integrating their perspectives into organisational strategies. Organisations can develop more targeted and impactful communication approaches by understanding how the public functions as dynamic partners within the system. In conjunction with theories such as Chay-Nemeth's theory of publics (discussed below), systems theory provides a broad structure for achieving successful SDG communication. The Grow It Yourself (GIY) movement, established in 2008, presents a compelling case study of how the systems theory of public can be applied to address complex global problems. GIY demonstrated the power of interconnectedness to achieve SDG 2 – Zero Hunger by fostering a network of individuals, organisations, and media outlets. GIY's initiatives prioritise inclusivity and accessibility, empowering individuals to participate actively in creating a more sustainable food system. Programmes like the 'Grow Cook Eat' kit box and collaborations with RTÉ, Ireland's national broadcaster, strategically target a broad public to raise awareness and promote sustainable food practices.

The organisation's focus on education and community-driven action stems from adopting an open systems framework. This perspective acknowledges that transformative change originates at the individual level within interconnected communities. Its alignment with SDG 2 and partnership with the SDG 2 Advocacy Hub underscore the movement's understanding of how these open networks influence policy and global action. This systems-level approach is essential for creating lasting solutions to complex challenges like food insecurity and underscores the continual need for active engagement. Publics constantly evaluate organisational actions, communicating their perceptions through media coverage, social media, and other channels. Organisations must be receptive to this feedback to maintain positive public relationships and adapt their approach accordingly. The GIY case study highlights the critical role of information flow, which fosters trust and builds strong connections between organisations and their public.

Public Engagement & Communication Strategies: A Synergy of Dewey & Situational Theory for Communicating the SDGs

In his situational theory of publics (STP), James Grunig challenged the notion of a monolithic general public. Instead, he proposed that publics are formed based on their level of involvement and stake in an issue or organisation. The formation and behaviours of the public, particularly in response to social, political, and organisational matters, pose a complex challenge to those in the field of communication. John Dewey, a prominent American philosopher and sociologist, provided foundational insights into the nature of publics. Building upon this work, Grunig refined these concepts into the Situational Theory of Publics (STP). This influential theory offers PR professionals a unique tool for understanding how publics emerge and functions when faced with specific problems or situations (Grunig, 1997).

The core premise of STP suggests that publics are not inherent or predetermined entities. Instead, they merge based on situational factors, namely the degree to which individuals recognise a problem, feel involved with the issue, and perceive their capacity to influence its resolution (Grunig, 1997). STP categorises publics as latent, aware, or active, reflecting increasing problem recognition and action levels. The variables of problem recognition, constraint recognition, and level of involvement are crucial in determining the potential activity of a given public. By understanding different publics' underlying motivations and constraints, communicators can strategically tailor their messages and engagement strategies. Effective communication is tailored not just to the issue itself but to the level of awareness, involvement, and constraints of the specific audience being addressed.

Grunig's and Dewey's philosophical pragmatism offers valuable insights into adopting a PR strategy that works to advance the SDGs. STP provides a framework for understanding how publics form and act based on their awareness and engagement levels. The concept of the public emerging from shared problems offers a starting point that seeks to engage diverse stakeholders. By understanding the ways that potential publics form around issues such as environmental concerns, fair labour practices, and social justice, PR can proactively establish open communication channels to foster mutually beneficial dialogue. In this context, situational theory offers a complementary dimension by segmenting the public based on their awareness (latent, aware, active) level of specific SDGs. PR is better equipped to facilitate constructive dialogue between organisations and the public by emphasising two-way discourse. Therefore, open and timely communication is essential for latent publics with limited SDG awareness, and campaigns employing clear, concise language can thus create mutual understanding. The aware public may benefit from more in-depth information presented *via* white papers or media partnerships highlighting solutions and their potential impacts. Active publics often seek greater involvement and can be engaged through participatory platforms, such as online forums or collaborative initiatives.

Human trafficking, a complex global issue undermining SDG 16 – Peace, Justice & Strong Institutions, demands ongoing public engagement. The *Anyone* campaign analysed in this book demonstrates a strategic application of STP by targeting diverse segments of the population to raise awareness and combat hate crimes. Through its multifaceted approach, including a short film, website, and social media presence, the campaign connects with publics who demonstrate varying levels of problem recognition and involvement concerning human trafficking. By emphasising the potential victimisation of anyone, the campaign addresses the situational context and combats the misconception that human trafficking solely impacts marginalised groups. This broader framing expands public concern and motivation to act. The campaign's initial success suggests the potential for an even more significant impact. Integrating a more targeted social media strategy on platforms like Instagram could mean reaching a wider audience and significantly younger demographics. Additionally, expanding collaborations with NGOs and stakeholders could amplify the campaign's message, resources, and potential for transformative change.

The integration of Dewey and STP compels PR professionals to navigate complex communication dynamics. Persuasion-oriented tactics must make way for fostering dialogue that acknowledges public agency. Additionally, it is critical to recognise power imbalances and strive for strategies that empower all voices within the public sphere. Finding the right balance between deliberation and decisive action, particularly when addressing urgent SDG challenges, requires careful consideration. Combining Dewey's emphasis on public formation and dialogue with STP's focus on targeted communication provides PR professionals with a valuable framework for SDG advocacy. This approach promotes genuine engagement, strengthening relationships, meaningful contributions, and a healthier public sphere (Dewey, 1927).

Grunig's Four Models: A Cornerstone of Public Relations

Grunig's four models of PR provide a foundational framework for understanding how organisations approach communication. These models – press agentry / publicity, public information, two-way asymmetrical, and two-way symmetrical – represent a spectrum progressing from one-way information dissemination towards dialogue-based engagement (Grunig, 1984). The evolution from the early focus on persuasion to the emphasis on mutual understanding in the two-way symmetrical model aligns with the shift towards more participatory communication strategies demanded by the complex goals of the SDGs. While the linearity of Grunig's model can be critiqued, its enduring relevance lies in its ability to help practitioners assess their communication approaches.

Understanding publics as active stakeholders is fundamental in applying Grunig's four models to create messages that resonate with target audiences and gain legitimacy. The audience's varying knowledge, interest, and involvement are critical factors in tailoring effective engagement strategies. While Grunig's models offer a valuable starting point, it is essential to acknowledge the inherent power imbalances in communication. Dewey and Chay-Nemeth both emphasised the importance of public deliberation alongside the consideration of historical conditions that constrain dialogue, and this emphasis is vital in building truly inclusive communication strategies (Dewey, 1927; Chay-Nemeth, 2001).

The WorkEqual campaign for gender equality in the Irish workplace offers a compelling example of how Grunig's STP can be strategically applied to achieve social change. The campaign's communication efforts closely align with critical aspects of Grunig's framework. Events like the *Equal Pay Day* seminar with diverse guest speakers demonstrate the campaign's commitment to two-way communication. This exchange of information allows for a nuanced understanding of public concerns and facilitates the development of tailored messaging. Furthermore, the campaign's focus on strategic publics is evident. *Equal Pay Day* purposefully targets women in the workforce, a public directly impacted by the gender pay gap. Including policymakers also suggests a deliberate attempt to influence a separate decisionmaking public.

The campaign highlights the importance of relationship building, a central tenet of Grunig's theory. Securing major sponsorships with organisations such as Primark indicates efforts to cultivate relationships within influential corporate sectors, potentially leading to increased resources and greater campaign reach. However, the campaign's initial struggles to secure sponsorships underscore advocacy groups' ongoing challenges regarding long-term funding – a common obstacle highlighted in Grunig's model. Overall, the WorkEqual campaign demonstrates the effectiveness of Grunig's STP in driving social change. By prioritising two-way communication, strategically engaging with different publics, and actively building relationships, the campaign has raised awareness, influenced policy discussions, and made significant strides towards promoting gender equality in the Irish workforce.

The *Hate Crime Hurts Us All* campaign in Ireland is another compelling case study for understanding the application of Grunig's four models. This initiative, spearheaded by the Coalition Against Hate Crime Ireland and the social marketing agency We The People, strategically engaged the public in advocating for dedicated hate crime legislation – the campaign's framework aligned with Grunig's model by emphasising two-way symmetrical communication. A comprehensive survey of diverse minority communities informed the campaign's messaging, ensuring it reflected the lived experiences of those affected by hate crimes. This approach highlights Grunig's emphasis on asymmetrical information exchange for understanding public concerns and effectively tailoring communication. Focusing on strategic publics is another critical aspect of the campaign's success. Impactful out-of-home advertisements featuring real individuals sought to raise awareness among the general public and garner widespread support. Additionally, collaborations with influencers amplified the message, extending the campaign's reach. This strategic approach displays the importance of relationship building in Grunig's theory, as these partnerships significantly broadened the campaign's impact.

Grunig's four models, coupled with an understanding of publics as dynamic stakeholders, equip communication professionals with a powerful toolkit. Employing these models enables the design of targeted messages that resonate with specific audiences, fostering public participation and a sense of shared responsibility. Additionally, it allows for adapting communication strategies in response to complex and evolving issues. Effective communication informed by these models and a nuanced understanding of publics ultimately empowers communities, influences policymakers, and accelerates progress towards a more sustainable and equitable future.

Chay-Nemeth's Theory of Publics: A Framework for Public Relations & SDG Communication

Constance Chay-Nemeth (2001) pointed out that the notion of the public as a singular, monolithic entity has been challenged by PR scholars who argue for the need to recognise the diversity and complexity of publics. Botan & Hazleton (2006) echoed this sentiment, stating "Public relations practitioners must recognise that there is no single 'general public' but rather a variety of publics, each with its own needs, interests, and communication preferences". Chay-Nemeth's (2001) dynamic theory of publics advances the field of PR by shifting from the view of audiences as passive recipients to recognising their active role in shaping issues and driving solutions. This resonates powerfully with the core purpose of the UN SDGs, which seek to address collective global challenges.

Chay-Nemeth's theory departs from traditional audience segmentation and emphasises the power dynamics between messenger and receiver. She classified the public into four distinct groups based on their social capital, which centred on three historical conditions – resource dependency, discursive connectivity, and legitimacy – and four categories of publics: circumscribed, co-opted, critical, and circumventing. This understanding enables PR practitioners to develop effective strategies that resonate with stakeholders and help address evolving concerns. By prioritising common issues over general demographic classifications, communicators can better identify specific groups unified around common interests (for example, environmentalists and advocates for ethical supply chains). This allows for creating communication that speaks directly to the values of these issue-driven publics. Communication strategies, therefore, must remain flexible to maintain relevance and impact, ensuring that messaging remains timely and aligned with evolving public sentiment.

In advocating for the minimum unit pricing (MUP) policy, Alcohol Action Ireland (AAI) strategically employed concepts central to Chay-Nemeth's theory of public by targeting politicians as a critical public. It presented evidence supporting MUP's effectiveness alongside polling data demonstrating public support, which aimed to influence political decisionmaking and secure commitment to the Public Health Alcohol Act (PHAA). However, as Chay-Nemeth posited, power imbalances within the public can hinder marginalised voices. This proved a challenge for AAI, as the extensive access and influence of the drinks industry threatened to overshadow their advocacy efforts.

Despite resource constraints, they navigated this complex power dynamic. The drinks industry's influence, including funding for seemingly neutral organisations like Drinkaware, exemplifies the challenges public health advocates face. AAI's dissemination of accurate information about MUP through its website and social media channels fostered a more informed public. Their emphasis on MUP's targeted impact on the cheapest, most potent drinks while posing minimal effect on low-risk drinkers sought to reshape the dominant narratives put forward by the alcohol industry. Furthermore, AAI's use of personal testimonies, such as *David's Story*, powerfully highlighted the links between alcohol, mental health, and suicide. It ran in tandem with extensive media outreach that further broadened the influence of AAI's message. This approach resonates with Chay-Nemeth's emphasis on amplifying marginalised voices and lived experiences to challenge dominant narratives.

Promoting complex goals like the SDGs demands particularly nuanced communication. Chay-Nemeth's perspective offers valuable insight that emphasises the public's interconnected nature, highlighting the shared responsibility in encouraging broad-based SDG participation. As evidenced by the case studies presented in this book, the strategic use of a multifaceted media mix encompassed social media platforms, established communication channels, and directed community engagement initiatives demonstrably fostered inclusivity, maximised audience reach, and cultivated opportunities for productive dialogue.

Publics are powerful evolving entities, coalescing around shared concerns and with a membership constantly evolving as issues gain or lose salience, often driven by communication. The presence of internal diversity of viewpoints further compounds the inherent complexity of the public. Effective communication strategies must, therefore, be tailored to resonate with these distinct segments of the broader public. Furthermore, PR strategies must possess high skill and adaptability to address the ever-changing nature of publics. Issues constantly evolve, and new publics emerge, necessitating a fluid approach. As Heath (1998) posited, the true power of communication lies in its ability to shape discourse within the public sphere. Organisations can leverage communication to either reinforce or challenge existing power structures.

The communication strategies employed for the SDGs can either solidify existing power structures or function as a catalyst for transformative change. This outcome hinges on how these strategies address power dynamics, particularly by ensuring meaningful participation from diverse voices. Chay-Nemeth (2001) emphasised preventing dominant narratives from marginalising those with fewer resources. Effective SDG messaging should encourage productive dialogue within key publics, fostering a shift from mere awareness-raising to collaborative problem-solving. Publics and their concerns are constantly evolving, necessitating agile communication approaches. Reconciling divergent viewpoints within the public requires a nuanced strategy and a commitment to long-term dialogue.

Leveraging Linkage Theory for Effective SDG Communication

In their 1984 publication, Todd Hunt and James Grunig offered a framework for understanding and managing the relationships between organisations and their stakeholders. This is today referred to as linkage theory (Grunig & Hunt, 1984), and it posits that organisations have four different linkages with different categories of publics: functional, normative, diffused, and enabling. Looking at the three fundamental forms of linkages and their roles in SDG communication, we can develop a communication strategy characterised by varying degrees of connection to the different strata of the public to be targeted, as the examples below indicate.

- **Functional linkages:** Functional linkages facilitate an organisation's core operations by exchanging information and resources with critical stakeholders, including employees, suppliers, and consumers;
- **Normative linkages:** Grounded in mutual values and objectives, these linkages connect organisations with entities such as NGOs, industry groups, and community organisations dedicated to sustainability causes;
- **Diffused linkages**: These less formal connections with the broader public often manifest through media relations, social media interactions, or sponsorships designed to cultivate a favourable public image and brand association with sustainability.

Linkage theory complements the previous alternative theories, offering PR practitioners a road map to designing SDG communication strategies that promote public participation, collaboration, and support for sustainable initiatives. Key to this theory is the emphasis on establishing strong, reciprocal relationships between organisations and their diverse publics. Unlike traditional persuasion models, linkage theory positions the public as active stakeholders with a vested interest in an organisation's actions and achieving aligned SDG targets. When applying this framework, it is essential to consider internal publics (employees, investors) and external ones (customers, communities, NGOs).

Leave No Trace Ireland's *Love This Place, Leave No Trace* campaign showcased the application of the linkage theory of publics for raising environmental awareness.

By strategically identifying connections between the environment and distinct audiences, the campaign aimed to influence outdoor recreational behaviour effectively. Leave No Trace Ireland's research pinpointed specific linked publics. The campaign's initial focus on the general public, including those new to outdoor recreation, evolved in 2023 to a refined strategy targeting the 18 to 34 demographic. This evolution demonstrated the organisation's commitment to understanding these linked relationships, acknowledging each public's unique connections with the environment. It began by addressing littering, a widespread behaviour with negative impacts – the subsequent shift towards broader responsible outdoor practices aligned better with the needs of the younger target demographic. Leave No Trace Ireland skilfully adapts its communication channels to engage these distinctly linked publics. Radio and television reach a broad audience, while social media and influencer collaboration (Rozanna Purcell) specifically connect with younger individuals. Campaign metrics – including radio reach and social media impressions – and recognitions like the Charity Impact Award illustrate the campaign's success in establishing initial linkages and promoting awareness. Furthermore, annual refinements and initiatives such as the national *Love This Place Day* demonstrate Leave No Trace Ireland's ongoing commitment to developing stronger connections with specific audiences.

At the core of linkage theory lies the establishment of strong, mutually beneficial relationships. These relationships necessitate a comprehensive understanding of stakeholder needs and expectations, a commitment to transparent communication, and a clear demonstration of social responsibility. Organisations establish a solid foundation for mobilising public support and engagement with the SDGs by cultivating trust and understanding. Through building trust-based relationships, promoting collaboration, and tailoring communication to diverse publics, organisations can become powerful catalysts for broader SDG engagement and ultimately contribute to creating a more sustainable future.

Conclusion

Successful implementation of SDG communication strategies, as demonstrated by the case studies presented in this book, necessitates moving beyond perceiving audiences as passive information recipients. For effective sustainable communication, a strategic synthesis of the Grunig and Hunt model with both situational and systems theories offers a robust framework. This integrated approach, while acknowledging the power dynamics highlighted by Chay-Nemeth's theory, provides valuable tools for tailoring communication efforts. By prioritising relationship networking through embedding enabling and functional linkages, organisations create an environment that is conducive to the long-term success of sustainability initiatives.

In order to realise the ambitious vision of the SDGs, robust public understanding and engagement are essential. Sustainability communication must transcend policymaking and serve as a powerful tool for outreach and stakeholder dialogue (United Nations, 2015). Deciphering how diverse publics conceptualise sustainability allows organisations to craft messages that resonate, promoting acceptance and encouraging wider dissemination. Sustainability's evolution from a buzzword to a global imperative demands a strategic communication approach that must acknowledge the power of dominant stakeholders, prioritise a deep understanding of diverse publics, and employ a flexible approach to the communication models discussed above. Through collaboration and tailored messaging, organisations can champion sustainability initiatives that drive meaningful, long-term change. While the SDGs provide a foundational framework, effective sustainability communication based on public engagement is the catalyst needed to achieve their full potential. To maximise impact, communicators should take the following actions:

- **Identify relevant publics (Chay-Nemeth and systems theory):** Following Chay-Nemeth (2001) and systems theory principles, the first step involves identifying key stakeholders for each SDG (for example, communities, businesses, governments). A systemic understanding of their interconnected roles is crucial;
- **Understand public concerns (Chay-Nemeth):** Building on Chay-Nemeth's (2001) emphasis on stakeholder needs, this stage entails comprehending the specific interests, needs, and potential hesitations of each public, acknowledging the heterogeneity within each group;
- **Choose the right Grunigian model:** Depending on the target public and the communication goals, a two-way asymmetrical or symmetrical approach from Grunig's model (1984) may be most suitable;
- **Craft tailored messages (systems theory and Chay-Nemeth):** Drawing on systems theory and Chay-Nemeth (2001), this stage involves developing messages that resonate with the specific concerns of each public, while also addressing the interconnectedness of the SDGs;
- **Facilitate dialogue and collaboration (Chay-Nemeth & Grunig):** Inspired by Chay-Nemeth (2001) and Grunig (1984), this step focuses on creating opportunities for public participation in discussions and solution finding, fostering a sense of shared ownership over the SDGs.

Real-world challenges, such as limited resources or countering dominant greenwashing narratives, must be proactively addressed. A multifaceted and integrated communication strategy is crucial for effective SDG communication. It is important to note that the various theoretical frameworks are not mutually exclusive but rather complementary and should be employed in tandem. For instance, Chay-Nemeth's theory complements both systems theory and Grunig's four models of PR. Systems theory focuses on the organisation–public relationship, while Chay-Nemeth's work delves deeper into the power structures between the messenger and publics, enabling more targeted communication.

This combined understanding is vital for strategic SDG advocacy, which depends on comprehending power dynamics, tailoring messages, and fostering genuine dialogue.

Implementing this multifaceted approach involves overcoming some potential obstacles. Sustainability communication must consciously reach marginalised and disempowered audiences to ensure broad representation through collaboration, which often necessitates navigating conflicting perspectives among stakeholders. Communication strategies must therefore remain responsive to the ever-evolving sustainability landscape and changing public priorities. In conclusion, by integrating stakeholder theory, systems theory, and the Grunig model, this framework offers a road map for strategic public engagement in SDG communication. Understanding public views is essential for crafting targeted messages that resonate with diverse audiences. Furthermore, fostering dialogue and collaboration is crucial for generating innovative solutions and achieving the SDGs in a sustainable manner.

References

Bain, P.G., Kroonenberg, P.M., Johansson, L.O., Milfont, T.L., Crimston, C.R., Kurz, T., Bushina, E., Calligaro, C., Demarque, C., Guan, Y. & Park, J. (2019). Public views of the Sustainable Development Goals across countries. *Nat Sustain 2*, pp.819–825. https://doi.org/10.1038/s41893-019-0365-4.

Botan, C.H. & Hazleton, V. (eds.). (2006). *Public Relations Theory II*. New York: Lawrence Erlbaum Associates.

Chay-Nemeth, C. (2001). Revisiting publics: A critical archaeology of publics in the Thai HIV/AIDS issue. *Journal of Public Relations Research*, 13(2), pp.127–161.

Deacon, B. (2016). Assessing the SDGs from the point of view of global social governance. *Journal of International & Comparative Social Policy*, 32(2), pp.116–130. https://doi.org/10.1080/21699763.2016.1198266.

Dewey, J. (1927). *The Public & Its Problems: An Essay in Political Inquiry*. Chicago: Swallow.

Grunig, J.E. (1997). A Situational Theory of Publics: Conceptual History, Recent Challenges & New Research. In: D. Moss, T. MacManus & D. Vercic (eds.), *Public Relations Research: An International Perspective* (pp.3–48). London: International Thomson Business Press.

Grunig, J.E. & Grunig, L.A. (2000). Public relations in strategic management and strategic management of public relations: Theory and evidence from the IABC Excellence Project. *Journalism Studies*, 1(2), pp.303–321. https://doi.org/10.1080/1461670050028271.

Grunig, J.E. & Hunt, T. (1984). *Managing Public Relations*. New York: Holt, Rinehart & Winston.

Grunig, James E. (1984). Organisations, environments, and models of public relations. *Public Relations Research & Education*, 1(1), pp.6–29.

Heath, R. (1998). *Crisis Management for Managers & Executives*. London: Pearson Education.

Livesey. S.M. (2001). Eco-identity as discursive struggle: Royal Dutch Shell, Brent Spar, and Nigeria. *Journal of Business Communication*, 38(1), p.61.

Mitchell, R.K., Agle, B.R. & Wood, D.J. (1997). Toward a theory of stakeholder identification and salience: Defining the principle of who and what counts. *Academy of Management Review*, 22(4), pp.853–886. https://doi.org/10.2307/259247.

Rosenau, J.N. (1984). A pre-theory revisited: World politics in an era of cascading interdependence. *International Studies Quarterly*, 28(3), pp.245–305.

Schramm, W. (1954). *The Process & Effects of Mass Communication*. Urbana: University of Illinois Press.

United Nations (2015). *Transforming Our World: The 2030 Agenda for Sustainable Development*. Retrieved from United Nations Department of Economic and Social Affairs, Sustainable Development: https://sdgs.un.org/2030agenda.

IX. SDG 8 – Decent Work & Economic Growth
Caritas Czech Republic's *Meaningful Gift* Campaign

Gabriela Doleckova

Abstract

This case study examines Caritas Czech Republic's *Meaningful Gift* campaign from the perspective of SDG 8, which recognises the importance of sustained economic growth and high levels of economic productivity by creating well-paid quality jobs and calls for opportunities for full employment and decent work for all. The campaign aims (among other things) to enhance the economic self-sufficiency of individuals in developing nations through education and vocational training. The study explores campaign elements, from its mission alignment with SDG 8 to tactics such as social media engagement and media exposure. Although the campaign successfully raises funds and awareness, it needs to explicitly communicate the SDGs, instead opting for a human-centric approach. The results show positive media coverage and increased engagement. However, a critical analysis suggests potential limitations in opting out of leveraging the SDGs for communication.

Introduction

The transition from the UN Millennium Development Goals to the SDGs marked a departure from the developed-developing country dichotomy towards universal aspirations. Despite the SDGs' inclusive vision, inequality and poverty persist alarmingly. The SDG 2023 report presents a concerning projection: if current developmental trends continue, by 2030 approximately 575 million people will live in extreme poverty, while only one in three nations are expected to achieve their goal of reducing national poverty levels by half. The SDGs aim to benefit all individuals regardless of their background or location. However, bridging socio-economic gaps presents significant challenges.

Humanitarian not-for-profit organisations have always been committed to improving living conditions and livelihoods. Even before the conceptualisation of the SDGs, these organisations worked tirelessly to uplift communities. While governments and the UN play a vital role in spearheading the SDGs, the active participation of diverse entities such as businesses and non-governmental organisations (NGOs) is fundamental to broadening their scope and impact.

This case study focuses on the *Meaningful Gift* campaign run by the international division of Caritas Czech Republic. The campaign operates with a focused mission: to raise funds to promote individuals' economic self-sufficiency in developing countries. This goal is achieved by promoting education and vocational training, which aligns with SDG 8's goal of ensuring decent work and promoting economic growth for all. The UN SDGs provide a comprehensive framework to address global challenges, most notably economic prosperity, social inclusion, and environmental sustainability. Within this framework, SDG 8 aims to promote sustained, inclusive, and sustainable economic growth while ensuring complete and productive employment for all. It outlines specific targets, ranging from GDP growth and supportive policies to the eradication of modern slavery and the enforcement of labour rights.

The SDG 2023 report highlights the urgent need for accelerating the initiatives with the UN noting that one in four young people in less developed countries does not have any form of education, employment, or training. The statistics in the report reflect the prevalence of precarious working conditions and a significant gender gap; therefore, the pursuit of economic growth and decent work should be at the forefront of the UN's ongoing development efforts. However, recent data on SDG 8's progress has recorded one of the highest levels of stagnation / regressions of all goals and has yet to progress. The *Meaningful Gift* campaign's efforts to empower individuals in developing countries through education and vocational training underscores the critical role of humanitarian organisations in advancing the agenda of sustainable economic growth and decent work.

About the Campaign

The *Meaningful Gift* campaign, organised by the Humanitarian & Development Aid Department of Caritas Czech Republic, is an annual Christmas initiative. Caritas Czech Republic, a prominent non-profit organisation in the Czech Republic, orchestrates the campaign, which allows individuals to make donations on behalf of others, providing an ideal platform to participate in non-material gift-giving during the holidays. Unlike traditional Christmas campaigns, the *Meaningful Gift* campaign offers various categories on the Caritas website under the themes of health, self-sufficiency, education, environment, and humanitarian aid. This unique structure allows donors to select gifts that reflect their preferences, making giving more personal and purposeful.

Recognising the urgent need to address youth unemployment and the precarious employment situations faced by vulnerable groups in developing nations, as highlighted in the SDG 2023 report, Caritas Czech Republic brings solutions across multiple countries. From vocational training to third-level education, internship placement, and financial literacy training, Caritas Czech Republic helps people alleviate economic precarity through sustainable professional progress. Many of these invaluable projects are financed through the purchase of Christmas vouchers, which become accessible to individuals in most need.

The *Meaningful Gift* campaign offers services empowering people with business skills and financial literacy, enabling them to establish businesses and achieve self-sufficiency. It also provides vocational training, such as sewing and beekeeping, as well as support for after-school education and grants for higher education. The campaign's website (https://svet.charita.cz/en/donate-hadc/a-meaningful-gift/) presents these offerings and features stories of Caritas Czech Republic's concrete actions in these communities. These stories highlight real individuals whose lives have been positively transformed by the aid provided through these gifts, ensuring sustainable livelihoods. The initiative by Caritas Czech Republic offers practical solutions to vulnerable individuals or marginalised communities, such as widows or refugees, who often face limited career prospects. It presents a pathway to independence and a sustainable means to overcome long-term poverty. One of the beneficiaries featured is 25-year-old Laurinda from Angola, who fled to Zambia. A single mother of three, she lives in a Zambian refugee settlement with low prospects for employment. Thanks to a sewing course Caritas provided, she is now a successful seamstress with a stable income. Not only does people's ability to make a living benefit them, but it also serves their community as they provide necessary services.

Primarily a fundraising effort, the campaign also serves as a catalyst to raise awareness of Caritas's work to address pressing global issues, particularly the challenge of securing a sustainable livelihood in developing countries. Caritas Czech Republic, a well-established organisation recognised by national and international bodies such as the Czech Development Agency, the European Commission and various UN development agencies, relies on diverse sources of income to finance these ambitious projects. While institutional funding is most of its support, individual contributions, raised through initiatives such as the *Meaningful Gift* campaign, enable the NGO to provide aid independently and flexibly.

Beyond its fiscal goals, the campaign has significant public relations potential. Despite being a newly established department with only a few years of experience, the public relations team of Caritas Czech Republic's international division have managed to raise the profile of the *Meaningful Gift* campaign by capitalising on the existing demand for gift certificates as an alternative to material gifts. This strategic focus has significantly helped strengthen the visibility and reach of the NGO and increased its presence in the public both at home and abroad.

Tactics & Activities

The *Meaningful Gift* campaign uses a diverse approach across various communication channels, including both paid and unpaid media exposure. The organisation's social media platforms and website are critical to the communication strategy. Caritas Czech Republic actively uses Facebook, Instagram, and Twitter / X, regularly posts blog updates on its website, and highlights the campaign in monthly newsletters. On social media, Caritas continuously highlighted examples of tangible help the *Meaningful Gift* can provide and encouraged people to donate. The public relations team continuously shared compelling stories of people whose lives have been improved with the help of Caritas Czech Republic. Complementing these efforts, the campaign secures visibility through unpaid media, appearing in news articles, interviews, and blog mentions. They appeared in several interviews, such as appearances on the national Czech TV and TV Noe, a Christian TV channel. It also used the Czech webpage for Giving Tuesday's global initiative to promote the *Meaningful Gift*. In addition, the 2023 edition of the campaign uses social media advertising on platforms such as Facebook and Instagram and the 'Sklik' advertising tool on the popular Czech search engine 'Seznam.cz'.

The campaign also extends its reach through physical installations such as the *Meaningful Gift* exhibition, strategically placed in busy hubs such as T-Mobile's headquarters in Prague. This exhibition tells the stories of people whose lives have been changed by these gifts and features an easily accessible QR code for convenient donations. In an interview for this book, Lenka Pipková, Caritas' Manager of Foreign Communication, noted that the exhibition had the opportunity to visit the Chamber of Deputies:

> This not only enabled individual politicians to contribute donations but also increased the visibility of Caritas as an organisation, giving credibility to our work. The involvement of these politicians in allocating grants and projects to various organisations ensures that Caritas remains a relevant institution for them in their decisionmaking processes.

The overarching goal of raising awareness of Caritas Czech Republic's work remains broad, and so does the target audience for the *Meaningful Gift* campaign. However, based on the experience of the first year of the campaign, the PR team has identified a cohort that is most likely to engage with their cause. In an interview, Lenka Chlubnová, online marketing specialist at Caritas Czech Republic, specified the target group as urban residents aged between 18 and 55, especially university alumni, as well as people who have previously interacted with Caritas' Facebook ads or visited its website.

The campaign emphasises the human element over the formal presentation of the SDGs, as Pipková emphasised that the intricacies of the SDGs may not resonate effectively with a broader audience:

> People don't get it. It's a very abstract thing for them. People are much more responsive to the story of someone who couldn't support themselves and Caritas helped them get around those difficulties and they can get on with their lives. Explaining some UN goals would not have such an effect.

Moreover, Pipková, commenting on the motivations behind Caritas work and its connection to SDG 8, added:

> We are going after the goals and what is needed to be done. We don't pick those projects because they fit a goal. However, all our work corresponds to that goal in some way.

Although the primary focus of the PR campaign does not emphasise the SDGs, Pipková noted that Caritas Czech Republic's efforts play a crucial role in advancing these global objectives. The Humanitarian & Development Aid Department of Caritas Czech Republic addresses SDGs only in a formal context, particularly in annual reports and materials for major donor agencies. Nevertheless, she further noted, its activities contribute significantly to visible and tangible achievements on the ground. Furthermore, Caritas has a specialised Global Education & Awareness division called Young Caritas, which focuses solely on social responsibility. This division runs initiatives such as the Dialogue 2030 project, which is specifically dedicated to raising awareness of sustainable development and promoting the SDGs. The campaign focuses on relatable narratives that showcase the transformative impact of charitable action, communicating with young people at an emotional level, and fostering positive engagement.

The deliberate decision to avoid explicit SDG communication in the campaign underlines Caritas Czech Republic's commitment to addressing the SDGs through practical interventions rather than simply aligning projects with pre-defined targets. This approach aligns with the organisation's ethos of prioritising real-impact projects, which has been shown to resonate with the public. The use of compelling personal stories curated by the charity has proven to be a more robust communication strategy than trying to highlight what, for many, can be seen as an abstract global goal. In essence, the *Meaningful Gift* campaign opts for a more emotive and personalised approach. It seeks to evoke empathy and achieve positive responses by emphasising relatable human stories over the technical SDG narratives.

Results & Outcomes

Caritas' work and communication efforts have been a verified success, culminating in the Humanitarian & Development Aid Department of Caritas Czech Republic receiving a medal of merit from the Czech government this year. Pipková evaluated the campaign's success positively, based on the significant media coverage achieved from the previous year's *Meaningful Gift* initiative. The collective effect of continuous PR efforts is slowly bringing results, with mentions of the campaign appearing in online journals and on the radio, like Giving is good and the website of the Czech Bishops Conference, even before the start of the Christmas season.

Reassured by last year's return on investment (ROI), Pipková emphasised the ongoing nature of the campaign, which allows the PR team to evaluate previous results and update targeting strategies. For example, paid advertisements in public transport or magazines such as *Respekt* effectively increased visibility in the past year. However, it will not be used as a fundraising tool in the future as she recognised that the ROI on paid advertising in traditional media was not as high as they would like for this campaign. Nonetheless, the deliberate PR strategy and focus on offline presence over the past few years is beginning to pay off. She emphasised the importance of the organisation's visibility, as increased exposure correlates with greater public engagement and support for initiatives such as the *Meaningful Gift* campaign.

Setting objectives has played an essential part in the campaign's trajectory. In its initial year, the campaign aimed to address unmet market needs, secure funds, and raise public awareness of the work of the Humanitarian & Development Aid Department of Caritas Czech Republic. In the second year, the focus shifted towards transforming the *Meaningful Gift* into a viable fundraising mechanism with a targeted ROI of 150%. Additionally, the campaign aimed to increase the number of gift vouchers sold and to broaden the donor base. The 2023 *Meaningful Gift* campaign proved to be a resounding success in terms of the number of gifts and people purchasing, which increased by 181% compared to last year.

Moreover, Pipková pointed to a shift away from less profitable strategies, such as offline promotion on billboards, in the form of bus ads and ads in magazines. These proved expensive, and it is hard to derive their ROI. Instead, the PR team decided to capitalise on the online tools available and the awareness generated by the previous year's *Meaningful Gift* campaign and other sustained promotional activity throughout the year.

Although the exact fundraising outcomes are undisclosed, as fundraising activities operate independently of the PR team, the increase in web traffic indicates positive results. The significant growth in website visitors, attributed to multiple campaigns and humanitarian interventions, reflects positively on the overall effectiveness and resonance of Caritas Czech Republic's efforts. Moreover, the number of website visits significantly dropped from Christmas on, signifying that a large part of it was driven by the *Meaningful Gift* campaign.

Critical Analysis

The success of the *Meaningful Gift* campaign prompts a critical examination of its key strengths and potential areas for improvement. Several aspects contributed to the campaign's effectiveness. The timing of the campaign was aligned with the festive season, starting with Thanksgiving, a period associated with increased generosity and charitable giving. Research shows that 48% of people are more likely to donate during Christmas than any other time of the year. The fact that the campaign coincides with Christmas plays a crucial role in its success, as people often initiate a search for a campaign to donate to on someone's behalf. Therefore, the timing speaks to the strategy and effective use of the demand during the Christmas period.

The originality of the campaign may have played a role. Caritas Czech Republic distinguished itself by offering an innovative approach, expanding the narrative beyond traditional campaigns focusing on tangible gifts. The *Meaningful Gift* campaign introduced two distinct sections: self-sufficiency and education. These sections offered professional and academic training, enabling individuals to achieve economic independence, in a departure from conventional Christmas donation campaigns.

Although the campaign has achieved some positive successes, a few areas for improvement have been noted, which could substantially benefit future campaign strategies. The campaign should have used the SDGs in its communication. Studies show that the public, particularly the age group targeted by Caritas Czech Republic, is increasingly more aware of the SDGs. In 2020, 58% of the Czech population had never heard of SDGs; this number, however, decreased to 37% by 2022. Despite this, there is an emerging trend of diminishing engagement by NGOs, companies, and the private sector in communicating their SDG efforts. As highlighted by the Ipsos report on Czech awareness of SDGs, respondents noted a 9% drop in NGOs' SDGs communication. This omission by organisations highlights a significant gap in their ability to contribute to achieving SDGs and raise public awareness while profiting from the public's engagement with the topic.

The *Meaningful Gift* campaign offers a unique platform to promote the charity's long-term, sustainable solutions for improving lives in the developing world. By highlighting these efforts in its communication strategy, Caritas Czech Republic can stand out in the competitive fundraising market. This focus on long-term impact aligns with SDG 8, which aims to improve working conditions and create jobs for millions. While Caritas Czech Republic is already a significant organisation, integrating SDGs into its messaging could further amplify its positive impact. This could be achieved through the *Meaningful Gift* campaign or a separate SDG-focused initiative.

Conclusions

The *Meaningful Gift* campaign by Caritas Czech Republic is another iteration of the organisation's impactful work. However, the communication strategy presents an opportunity for improvement. Although the campaign aligns inherently with the ethos of the SDGs, the deliberate communication of these global objectives is absent from the campaign rhetoric. Caritas Czech Republic's PR management has yet to include explicit SDG-centred communication in individual-level campaigns such as the *Meaningful Gift*. However, analysis shows that the audience engaged by the campaign's paid media is actively interested in identifying and considering SDGs in organisational communication.

This presents an argument for Caritas Czech Republic to review its communication strategies. Incorporating SDGs into both individual and societal-level communications could yield significant benefits. As awareness of SDGs increases, particularly among the campaign's target audience, using SDG-focused narratives could improve resonance and engagement, such as through an SDG-centred campaign. Caritas Czech Republic can play a significant role in achieving the SDGs, raising societal awareness, and driving positive change by leveraging its influence and impact.

Explorations

1. Evaluate the effectiveness of Caritas Czech Republic's decision to prioritise human-centric stories over explicit communication of SDG 8 in the *Meaningful Gift* campaign.

2. What additional key performance indicators (KPIs) could be used to assess the campaign's impact on raising awareness, changing attitudes and contributing to SDG 8?

3. How could Caritas Czech Republic refine its audience segmentation to reach broader demographics and maximise the campaign's reach and impact?

4. The campaign used various communication channels, including social media, exhibitions, and interviews. Evaluate the effectiveness of these channels in reaching the target audience and achieving campaign objectives.

5. What communication tactics could Caritas Czech Republic employ to highlight the connection between its work and the goal of decent work and economic growth, while maintaining the emotional appeal of its storytelling?

X. SDG 10 – Reduced Inequalities
The Coalition Against Hate Crime Ireland
Hate Crime Hurts Us All Campaign

Tessa Thornton

Abstract

The *Hate Crime Hurts Us All* campaign, conducted by the Coalition Against Hate Crime Ireland (CAHCI) and We the People, exemplifies an impactful behaviour change initiative addressing the absence of dedicated hate crime legislation in Ireland. Aligned with SDG 10, the campaign adeptly tackled rising hate-related incidents, employing a multifaceted strategy involving a comprehensive survey, poignant out-of-home advertisements featuring real individuals, and strategic influencer engagement. Successful media outreach tactics, reaching approximately 7.4 million people, showcased the campaign's effectiveness in raising awareness and engaging diverse audiences. The survey was pivotal, providing compelling statistics that resonated across various media outlets. As Ireland moves towards implementing hate crime legislation, the campaign offers valuable insights, emphasising the importance of adapting strategies to an evolving societal context. Lessons learned, particularly regarding participant safety and influencer engagement, contribute to a nuanced approach in advocating for a more inclusive and equitable society.

Introduction

The *Hate Crime Hurts Us All* campaign was a behaviour change campaign led by CAHCI in response to the lack of definitive hate crime legislation in Ireland to highlight the ripple effect felt by minority communities when a hate crime or hate incident is committed against one of its members. The campaign was led in conjunction with We the People, a social marketing agency that specialises in behaviour change campaigns and assisting clients in targeting hard-to-reach audiences.

CAHCI is a civil society group made up of organisations representing demographics most often targeted by hate crime, which is currently defined by An Garda Síochána as "any criminal offence which is perceived by the victim or any other person to, in whole or in part, be motivated by hostility or prejudice, based on actual or perceived age, disability, race, colour, nationality, ethnicity, religion, sexual orientation or gender". CAHCI is chaired by the Irish Council for Civil Liberties (ICCL) and aims to enact meaningful reform of the law, policies, and practices relating to hate crime in Ireland.

The SDGs were established by the United Nations (UN) in 2015 as a part of the 2030 *Agenda for Sustainable Development*. They provide a comprehensive framework for individuals, organisations, and nations to address various social, economic, and environmental challenges to create a more sustainable and equitable world by 2030. This case study analysis examines how this campaign aligns with SDG 10, which is to "reduce inequality within and among countries", and, more specifically, how its activities and initiatives contribute to the achievement of Target 10.4, which is to "adopt policies, especially fiscal, wage, and social protection policies, and progressively achieve greater equality".

Background to Campaign

Prior to the establishment and launch of the campaign, two facts were identified and reiterated by the CAHCI: Ireland was one of the only countries in Europe that did not have specific and dedicated hate crime legislation, and that incidents of hate crime and violence were on the rise in Ireland. In 2021, it was found that there were 448 hate-related incidents and hate crimes recorded by An Garda Síochána, 389 of which were defined as hate crimes and 59 of which were recorded as 'non-crime hate-related incidents'.

As such, to understand the goals and strategies of the campaign and how they align with the initiatives of SDG 10, it is imperative to establish the backdrop against which it was developed: the rise of far-right groups and activities in Ireland. The country saw a surge of organised protests since 2020, as a digital pandemic populism mobilised various groups and individuals onto the streets. In particular, the misinformation associated with the roll-out of Covid-19 vaccines and implementation of Covid-related restrictions, coupled with the pervasive feelings of anxiety and isolation at the time, instilled unity and cohesivity within a previously fragmented far-right movement in Ireland. And this saw them quickly mobilised by ideas surrounding nativism, xenophobia, racism, homophobia, and rejection of scientific expertise.

Thirteen million posts taken from 1,640 online accounts over three years have been analysed by the Institute of Strategic Development. They indicate an exponential growth of misinformation and disinformation, particularly on platforms such as X (formerly Twitter), since the Covid-19 pandemic. A study carried out by the European Media & Information Fund suggests that the links created by the pandemic between various far-right groups have not disappeared since the pandemic was declared over. There have been exponential levels of unification over immigration and LGBTQI+-related issues, with research demonstrating a startling uptick in the use of terminology such as 'plantation', concerning immigrants and asylum seekers and 'groomers' relating to the LGBTQI+ communities. Such sentiments were seen as coming to a head in the so-called Dublin Riots, which took place in November 2023 following a knife attack outside a school, which resulted in the injuries of three children and one woman. A demonstration on the edge of the police barricade of the scene escalated into crowds of hundreds, some of whom were holding Tricolour flags and shouting "Irish lives matter". The riots saw the destruction of Gardaí vehicles and public transport links, and violence and looting caused a shutdown of the area and surrounding businesses for several days.

It is in this context that the Minister for Justice, Helen McEntee TD, announced that Oireachtas proceedings would commence regarding hate crime and hate speech legislation in late 2022 (the Bill entered its first stage in the Dáil on 1 November 2022). CAHCI stated its belief that the *Criminal Justice (Incitement to Violence or Hatred & Hate Crime) Bill 2022* would fill an ongoing gap in the Irish legal system. As such, CAHCI's goals for this campaign were established as increasing public understanding of what hate crime is, increasing understanding of how hate crime impacts vulnerable communities, showing the need for effective hate crime legislation, encouraging legislators to maintain a focus on hate crime; and calling for a national action plan to go beyond criminal law and address the roots of hate.

Tactics & Activities

As stated, the *Hate Crime Hurts Us All* campaign aimed to empower the target audiences to understand what hate crimes are, what classifies as hate crimes, and the impact that they have on minority communities. Furthermore, CAHCI wanted to show that hate crime can affect members of different communities in an intersectional way. Three pillars were central to the formation of this campaign: a survey, out-of-home advertisements, and the use of influencers and social media.

A snapshot survey was launched online, and over 400 members of various minority communities responded regarding their experiences and interactions with hate incidents within their communities. The survey was not segregated by singular identity to emphasise the intersectionality of minority groups and perception of the impact of such incidents, highlighting the aforementioned ripple effect upon which the campaign was focused. The data collected in the survey revealed that 65% of respondents felt anxious or depressed after a hate crime occurred within their community, 57% avoided neighbourhoods / streets where hate crimes occurred, and 35% altered the way they dressed following such incidents. In addition to this, 43% recorded themselves as having been the subject of a hate crime / hate incident, while 70% had heard or read about a hate incident involving a member of their community. As we examine the response to the campaign, we will see the integral role this survey played in the coverage of their activities.

The central pillar of the *Hate Crime Hurts Us All* campaign was their focus on out-of-home advertisements. The advertising campaign was unique in many ways because it featured real individuals from targeted communities to showcase the human impact of hate crime. Everyone featured had more than one minority identity, such as Pradeep Mahadeshwar, who is a gay man of colour, and Razan Ibraheem, who is a woman of migrant background. This again highlights the intersectionality and shared burden of hate crime. In capturing these creatives, the photographer, Vanessa Ifediora, guided them in reproducing the feelings and emotions evoked in their own experiences with hate incidents.

Central to the campaign was that the images were not violent or triggering to the public but instead evoked an emotional response based on people's lived experiences. Along with these images, the advertisements included statements about the individual, which sometimes featured statistics.

These images were displayed in strategic locations nationwide, such as on screens, billboards, and 34 washroom panels in Dublin, Galway, Cork, Waterford, and Limerick, to ensure their maximum reach. It was essential to the organisers that they could safely deliver their intended message and reach demographics they may not have ordinarily reached. Besides, they also enlisted influencers from minority communities to help generate interest and support for the campaign on their respective platforms. The influencers, such as Amanda Adé, Paddy Smyth, and Jacob Donegan, contributed by frequently posting to their social media pages the stories regarding updates to the campaign and petitions that could be signed to demonstrate support for the legislation. Also, We the People developed a social media toolkit and content calendar. This was circulated among coalition members to help them support the campaign and spread the word about any updates. This contained images for social media, draft posts that could be adapted for their various platforms, and a suggested posting frequency.

The campaign was launched on 12 September 2022, with a media event in the Kevin Kavanagh Art Gallery in Dublin city centre. Here, the images from the advertisements were displayed, and an array of speakers took part, moderated by the chairperson of CAHCI, Luna Liboni. Several national media outlets, academics, and representatives from the Department of Justice attended the event. Another key element of the event was the models from the advertisements who were in attendance spoke of their personal experiences with hate crimes and incidents and were available along with the chair for media interviews.

Results & Outcomes

One major result of the campaign launch event, and the activities leading up to it, was the impressive levels of media presence and attention it was able to garner on both local and national level. This included publications in the media outlets such as *The Irish Times*, the *Irish Daily Mail*, RTÉ, *District* magazine, and GCN. We the People used the launch as a content-gathering event to ensure momentum was maintained in the interim between the event and any legislative progress. Moreover, immediately following the event, the agency conducted multiple radio interviews across local and national levels, a key element in the political landscape in Ireland.

The level of media coverage garnered is important to behaviour change campaigns such as this one as they are less straightforward in measuring success levels within a campaign. As such, a key element in the success metrics for the *Hate Crime Hurts Us All* campaign was reach and awareness raising regarding the subject of hate crime. Through this lens, the campaign can be deemed a massive success. It culminated in a total reach of approximately 7.4 million people across the country, 1 million of whom were linked to the out-of-home advertisements, and 1.2 million as a result of campaigning on behalf of the chosen influencers. Additionally, it achieved over 400 signatures calling for a further action plan regarding hate crime and the requested legislation, which we mentioned as a key element of the CAHCI's campaign.

The survey included within the campaign was recognised as a key player in its success in garnering coverage and achieving such high reach levels. Publications such as GCN and *District* magazine, put a lot of focus on the proposed action plan outside of the legislation. This is because the story falls in line with the interests of their regular readership. Furthermore, the survey and the statistics the campaign provided became a hook for the national press outlets. These became their primary focus in the agency's coverage of the campaign. As such, it can be assumed that the campaign could not have been such a success without the use of this survey.

Critical Analysis

The campaign set out to raise awareness regarding the necessity for the implementation of dedicated hate crime legislation as part of a further action plan to tackle the issue of hate crime / incidents in Irish society. It framed hate crime as a societal problem – rather than a specific community problem – to achieve greater equality, thus aligning with SDG 10 and Target 10.4. This is especially evident in their out-of-home advertising. The selected locations generated heavy footfall from various people rather than places typically only frequented by specific communities. It can also be seen in the language used in the advertisements, which was inclusive rather than accusatory towards people outside of minority groups. It successfully demonstrated hate crimes as a universal issue, as evidenced by feedback to CAHCI.

A key element in analysing the activities of this campaign is identifying the differences between the context in which it was run and the context we find ourselves today. In the aftermath of the Dublin Riots and what they identified about Irish culture, we must question whether the campaign, despite its success, could be conducted in the same way now. Having individuals from minority groups represented in the campaign's imagery and hosting events wherein they share their first-hand experiences of hate crime in Ireland played a vital role in the campaign's poignancy and impact. However, the ease demonstrated recently in mobilising violent far-right groups would now have to be considered when you are advertising an event that centralises the experiences of minorities, particularly where it pertains to issues of immigration, sexuality, and gender expression. Furthermore, where the mental health of the creatives was of top priority to CAHCI in the formation of the campaign previously rather than physical safety, to conduct the same campaign today, both elements of the participants' well-being would have to be considered strongly.

On a separate note, when asked if any elements of the campaign would be conducted differently, viewing the campaign in the same context in which it took place, one area identified was the way the influencers were used. It was noted that there was a discrepancy or imbalance in how many times the influencers' followers viewed a video regarding a petition *versus* how many signatures the petition accrued from that platform. In other cases, it was noted that there was a lack of ease in accessing links to a petition. In the future, it should be ensured that there is ease of access in terms of message delivery, and concept expression. The language used should accurately reflect the influencers' respective audiences, to which the influencers could have input directly as they will have the best understanding of their followers.

Despite these considerations, by raising awareness, empowering marginalised communities, and calling for policy changes, the campaign directly addressed the goal of SDG 10, which is to reduce inequality, by promoting a more inclusive society and advocating for legal frameworks that could protect minorities in Ireland.

Conclusion

In conclusion, the *Hate Crime Hurts Us All* campaign acts as a compelling example of a behaviour change initiative addressing a critical societal issue. Set against the backdrop of a rising tide of hate-related incidents in Ireland and the absence of dedicated hate crime legislation, the campaign strategically aligned with SDG 10, which aims to reduce inequality within and among countries. The campaign's success is evident in its multifaceted approach, incorporating a comprehensive survey, impactful out-of-home advertisements featuring real individuals, and strategic use of social media influencers. By emphasising the intersectionality of hate crimes and their ripple effects on diverse communities, the campaign effectively garnered attention and engaged a broad audience. Crucially, the campaign achieved widespread media coverage, providing compelling statistics resonating with national and less mainstream media outlets. In addition, the campaign influenced public discourse, leading to over 400 signatures supporting a national action plan against hate crimes. While the campaign's success is evident, it is crucial to acknowledge the evolving context. The Dublin Riots underscore the need for a nuanced approach, considering potential threats to the safety of participants in events centred around minority experiences.

Furthermore, lessons learned from influencer engagement suggest refining strategies for maximum impact and accessibility. At present, the *Criminal Justice (Incitement to Violence or Hatred & Hate Offences) Bill* has been passed by Dáil Éireann and is currently before Seanad Éireann in its third stage as of 21 June 2023. As Ireland moves toward implementing hate crime legislation, this campaign is a pivotal moment in the fight against hate, advocating for a more inclusive and equitable society.

Acknowledgments

I want to express my sincere gratitude to Luna Liboni, Senior Policy Officer for the Irish Council for Civil Liberties and chair of the Coalition Against Hate Crime Ireland, whose insights on the campaign proved invaluable to my analysis of this case study.

Explorations

1. Discuss the potential benefits and drawbacks of broad and targeted PR strategies in the context of this campaign.

2. What ethical considerations should PR professionals prioritise when addressing sensitive and potentially polarising issues like hate crimes?

3. What qualitative or quantitative research methods could be employed to assess changes in public perception and understanding of the issue?

4. What new challenges and opportunities could arise after hate crime legislation is passed, and how should PR professionals adjust their approach accordingly?

5. What criteria should be used to select influencers, and how can their involvement be leveraged to maximise reach and engagement with diverse audiences?

XI. SDG 11 – Sustainable Cities & Communities

The Salthouse Hotel

David Little

Abstract

SDG 11 – Sustainable Cities & Communities aims to make cities and human settlements inclusive, safe, resilient, and sustainable. The Salthouse Hotel in Antrim, our case study for this chapter, offers a fascinating glimpse into how the tourism sector can embrace sustainability and contribute to SDG 11. Its innovative approach to implementing and communicating sustainable practices provides a valuable roadmap for other organisations striving to achieve this ambitious and crucial goal. With its commitment to sustainability, The Salthouse Hotel is an example of eco-friendly practices and social impact in the hospitality industry. This research will address three key questions. First, how does the hotel align with the targets and indicators of SDG 11; second, what are the benefits and challenges from a communications perspective of adopting a sustainability-oriented approach in the hospitality sector; and, finally, will the hotel inspire and influence other urban establishments to follow its example?

Introduction

In 2015, the UN adopted the 2030 *Agenda for Sustainable Development*, a global action plan for people, the planet, and prosperity. In this context, prosperity refers to economic growth, social development, and environmental protection. SDG 11 encompasses several targets and indicators, including:

11.1 Safe & Affordable Housing
11.2 Affordable & Sustainable Transport Systems
11.3 Inclusive & Sustainable Urbanisations
11.4 Protect the World's Cultural & Natural Heritage
11.5 Reduce the Adverse Effects of Natural Disasters
11.6 Reduce the Environmental Impact of Cities

11.7 Provide Access to Safe & Inclusive Green & Public Spaces
11.8 Implement Policies for Inclusion, Resource Efficiency & Disaster Risk Reduction.

The Salthouse Hotel's case study offers valuable insights, although it is essential to acknowledge its limitations. The hotel's unique context and location in rural Northern Ireland mean its specific communication strategies and outcomes may translate differently to other settings, particularly those outside the hospitality sector or in more urbanised environments. Furthermore, the complex topic of sustainable urban development is bound to generate diverse perspectives and interpretations. Thus, the findings presented in this chapter should be viewed as a starting point for further discussion and exploration rather than as definitive conclusions. Readers are encouraged to engage critically with the case study, considering its strengths and weaknesses in light of existing research and evidence. Doing so can foster a richer understanding of the challenges and opportunities involved in achieving SDG 11, paving the way for more effective communication strategies that drive sustainable urban development forward.

Background

Increasingly, customers are beginning to prioritise sustainable practices when choosing a hotel, even above price, location, and value for money. This aligns perfectly with the inspiration behind The Salthouse Hotel's sustainability campaign. Driven by their global travels and passion for sustainability, the owners recognised a growing demand for eco-conscious tourism. The front office manager, Claire Steele, explains: "Our directors witnessed first-hand the increasing importance of sustainability to customers worldwide. This fuelled their ambition to become Northern Ireland's first fully sustainable hotel. They meticulously researched global best practices and set ambitious goals to achieve this vision". This commitment to sustainability is evident in The Salthouse Hotel's emphasis on energy conservation, recycling, and greenscaping, which resonate strongly with environmentally conscious travellers.

In the evolving world of hospitality, sustainability is the new standard. Hotels like The Salthouse Hotel are pioneering luxurious, yet eco-conscious, accommodations, proving that indulgence and environmental responsibility can go hand in hand. However, challenges remain, especially in the realm of transportation. Transportation plays a pivotal role in the tourism and hotel industries but also presents a hurdle to achieving SDG 11's sustainability goals. The availability and accessibility of public transport significantly influence guest choices, favouring hotels near major hubs or with convenient connections. Yet, issues like traffic congestion and pollution cast a shadow on the guest experience, and the transport sector's carbon footprint further underscores the need for hotels to champion sustainable travel options.

Another crucial aspect of SDG 11 is addressing homelessness, a role that community-minded hotels like The Salthouse can uniquely contribute to. By offering shelter, food, and vocational training to those in need, hotels can uplift their communities and foster a sense of inclusivity. Such actions help individuals and align with the global agenda for sustainable urban development. While not all hotels have the capacity to offer long-term housing solutions for complex cases, they can provide temporary refuge through emergency accommodation, such as bed and breakfasts or family hubs. This goes beyond legal obligations, reflecting a growing movement towards corporate social responsibility and sustainable business practices. The Salthouse Hotel exemplifies this commitment to balancing economic success with positive social and environmental impact.

Tactics & Activities

The Salthouse Hotel's sustainability campaign is a dynamic, multi-faceted endeavour that engages stakeholders at every level and promotes eco-conscious practices. It is more than just a message; it is a collaborative effort to create a sustainable experience. The campaign focuses on guests, the primary recipients of the hotel's services. The Salthouse Hotel strives to provide memorable experiences that are both luxurious and environmentally responsible. Staff members are equally important, receiving comprehensive training on the hotel's sustainability initiatives, energy-saving measures, and innovative technologies. The Salthouse Hotel also reaches out to the broader public, showcasing its eco-friendly features to attract like-minded guests and encourage sustainable choices. This holistic approach fosters a sense of shared responsibility and empowers everyone involved to contribute to a greener future, the cornerstone philosophy of The Salthouse Hotel's sustainability success. As the face of the hotel, staff members receive a comprehensive induction, ensuring they are well-versed in the latest eco-friendly practices and can confidently communicate the hotel's sustainability ethos. This commitment to ongoing education empowers staff to deliver exceptional service that delights guests and strengthens the hotel's reputation.

The hotel's dedication to the local community extends to its suppliers, prioritising those who source and produce eco-friendly products and materials. This approach creates a ripple effect of economic benefits, as Steele emphasises: "We strive to keep everything we use as local as possible. It's about giving back and supporting our community". The Salthouse Hotel nurtures long-term, mutually beneficial relationships with local suppliers, bolstering the local economy and environment. To amplify its sustainability message, the hotel leverages a multi-channel approach, using social media platforms like Facebook, Instagram, and X (formerly Twitter) and local news outlets like the *Belfast Telegraph and Causeway & Antrim News*. The hotel shares its eco-friendly practices and achievements through engaging content on these platforms, attracting positive attention and reinforcing its commitment to sustainability. Its recent recognition with the 2023 Sustainability Award at the prestigious Georgina Campbell Irish Food & Hospitality Awards, which garnered widespread media coverage and social media buzz, exemplifies this strategy. Director Carl McGarrity's enthusiastic quotes about the award and the hotel's ambitious expansion plans further demonstrate The Salthouse's dedication to leading the way in sustainable hospitality.

By sharing its commitment to locally sourced and sustainable ingredients and its reliance on renewable energy sources, the hotel aims to attract positive attention and support the local economy and environment. Speaking about the importance of communicating the hotel's sustainability efforts, in particular, the use of locally sourced and sustainable ingredients and produce, with guests, Steele said, "It's really good to share that understanding with guests, that even when they're reordering, there are alternatives that can be good for the environment". The hotel operates solely on renewable energy, combining wind, solar power, and air-source heat pumps. This increases cost savings and reduces the hotel's carbon footprint.

The Salthouse Hotel's unwavering commitment to sustainability is evident in its operation, from staff training to procurement policies. The hotel thoroughly educates its employees on its eco-friendly practices and encourages them to share this knowledge with guests, fostering a culture of environmental awareness. The hotel's purchasing policy prioritises local and sustainable products, minimising its ecological footprint while reaping significant cost savings. To spread the word about its green initiatives, The Salthouse leverages Facebook, a popular platform among older audiences, to share engaging content highlighting its 'sustainable luxury' philosophy. Stunning photos and videos highlighting the hotel's eco-friendly infrastructure captivate followers, while celebrity visits, like those from Michael Fassbender and Pierce Brosnan, attract other demographics. The hotel adds a personal touch by featuring employees in its social media posts, forging a stronger connection with its audience and demonstrating its dedication to sustainability and its valued staff. The Salthouse Hotel's active engagement on Facebook, with over 39,000 likes and 41,000 followers, showcases the power of social media in amplifying its sustainability message and inspiring eco-conscious choices among its audience.

The hotel uses the 'Salthouse Mindset' to symbolise its commitment to creating a calm and relaxing environment, inviting guests to embrace this ethos when they arrive fully. The eco-friendly practices and luxurious amenities of the Salthouse Hotel reflect this mindset, encouraging guests to "leave it all behind and discover your coastal calm". This implies escaping the hustle and bustle of modern-day living and immersing oneself in the tranquil and natural beauty of the hotel's surroundings. The Salthouse Mindset also extends to the hotel's spa, where the staff are committed to creating escapism from the everyday pressures of busy life.

All of the treatments are designed to lower stress levels and improve well-being. The Salthouse Mindset promotes relaxation and well-being in an environmentally conscious way. The spa uses motion-sensor LED lighting powered by the hotel's self-generated energy. Through these proactive communication measures, The Salthouse Hotel showcases its commitment to sustainability and ensures that guests know these practices. By communicating its sustainability achievements effectively, the hotel promotes a culture of sustainability and encourages guests to adopt eco-friendly practices during their stay. This commitment to sustainability sets The Salthouse Hotel apart as a leader in eco-friendly hospitality.

The Salthouse Hotel's unwavering commitment to sustainability perfectly aligns with SDG 11, aiming to create inclusive, safe, resilient, and sustainable cities and communities. By prioritising renewable energy, sourcing local and eco-friendly products, and investing in staff training on sustainable practices, the hotel actively contributes to achieving SDG 11. These eco-conscious efforts minimise the hotel's environmental impact, promote sustainable tourism, and inspire guests to adopt similar practices during their stay. The hotel's effective communication further amplifies its impact. The Salthouse Hotel fosters a sustainability culture within its walls and beyond by sharing its sustainability journey and educating guests about eco-friendly choices.

Nigel McGrady, one of the hotel's directors, recognised the challenges of implementing sustainable practices in an area like Ballycastle and stressed that communication and education on the benefits of sustainable business practices play a significant role:

A lot of people are still learning about it, and they get quite angry if they see a windmill going up; it's important to educate them about using the wind and the sun because we can't rely on fossil fuel fields as we move forward. Everybody will be more socially responsible and educated about why we're doing it in the first place, but we have to do something.

McGrady also believes that businesses can receive financial benefits from pursuing these goals: "All businesses can save money by thinking just a little smarter about how they do things… so all businesses, if they think of it correctly, can benefit from saving in any kind of carbon neutral adventure".

Results & Outcomes

The Salthouse Hotel's investment in renewable energy sources has proven to be a remarkable success story. Its on-site wind turbine and solar panels generate enough electricity to power 150 homes annually, significantly reducing its carbon footprint and operational costs. Clean energy powers everything from motion-sensor LED lighting and efficient heat pumps to electric vehicle charging stations and even the hotel's electric kitchen. By incorporating innovative technology to monitor consumption, The Salthouse ensures optimal energy use, contributing more energy to the grid than it consumes. This impressive achievement demonstrates the hotel's dedication to sustainability and highlights the financial benefits of embracing eco-friendly practices. The significant cost savings from reduced energy consumption can be reinvested into other business areas, further enhancing guest experiences, and contributing to the local economy.

The Salthouse Hotel's commitment to sustainability has yielded many benefits for the hotel and the vibrant Ballycastle community. By prioritising local and eco-friendly suppliers, the hotel has reduced its environmental footprint and forged valuable relationships with local businesses, boosting the local economy and streamlining operations with shorter delivery times for essential items. A prime example of this symbiotic relationship is the hotel's partnership with RiverRidge, a local waste management company specialising in recycling. This collaboration ensures responsible waste disposal and propels The Salthouse closer to its zero-waste-to-landfill goal. The hotel's dedication to spreading its sustainability message has also reaped financial rewards, enabling a recent £1.2 million investment in a second restaurant, The Lookout. This exciting expansion enhances the hotel's offerings and creates 30 new jobs, further enriching the Ballycastle community.

Critical Analysis

The following analysis delves into how organisations effectively communicate their dedication to SDG 11. The Salthouse Hotel sets a high bar for transparency, offering detailed information on its website about its sustainability practices, including a comprehensive FAQ section and detailed descriptions of its eco-friendly rooms and spaces. However, there's always room for improvement. Imagine presenting this wealth of information in a more engaging and accessible format, like visually appealing infographics or informative videos. A dedicated section on the website could also make it easier for potential guests to discover the hotel's commitment to sustainability.

The communications strategy goes above and beyond by educating guests upon arrival about their eco-conscious initiatives and inviting them to embrace the 'Salthouse Mindset'. This raises awareness and empowers guests to make sustainable choices during their stay. To further enhance this educational aspect, the hotel could explore hosting interactive workshops or guided tours showcasing its impressive sustainability features, similar to innovative approaches from other eco-conscious establishments like Ashford Castle. Ashford Castle, for instance, has partnered with Winnow Solutions to leverage AI technology to reduce food waste, demonstrating a proactive approach to sustainability. Furthermore, its on-site wastewater treatment and waste monitoring systems highlight a holistic commitment to minimising environmental impact. By learning from such initiatives, The Salthouse Hotel can continue to evolve and enhance its already impressive sustainability efforts. The hotel's local and eco-friendly procurement policy supports the local economy and reduces the environmental impact of transportation. This aligns with SDG 11's aim to "support positive economic, social, and environmental links between urban, peri-urban, and rural areas by strengthening national and regional development planning". However, the hotel could communicate more about how this policy benefits Ballycastle's local community. Stakeholder theory posits that companies should consider not only their shareholders' interests but also those of a wider variety of stakeholders, such as suppliers, customers, and society at large, as doing so will lead to tremendous success.

SDG 11 envisions cities and communities that are inclusive, safe, resilient, and sustainable. While The Salthouse Hotel has demonstrated impressive strides in sustainability, there is an opportunity to expand its communication regarding inclusivity and resilience. For instance, showcasing how the hotel's facilities cater to all guests, including those with disabilities, would highlight its commitment to inclusivity. Additionally, highlighting preparations for potential environmental risks like extreme weather events, such as robust infrastructure and sustainable practices, would illustrate the hotel's dedication to resilience. Sharing these efforts through channels like sustainability reports, guest participation initiatives, and digital platforms could further amplify the hotel's positive impact. Inspired by the Shangri-La Hotel in Tokyo, renowned for its accessible luxury, The Salthouse could consider similar features like automatic doors and wheelchair-friendly layouts to ensure a welcoming experience for everyone.

One issue for the SDGs is the question of measurability and monitoring, and especially how to honestly and ethically communicate achievements where there is no agreed measurement metric. The Salthouse Hotel could improve its communication around this aspect by sharing how it measures and monitors its sustainability performance. For instance, it could share energy generation and consumption data, waste production and recycling, and other relevant metrics. This would demonstrate the hotel's commitment to accountability and provide tangible evidence of its sustainability achievements. Documents related to environmental, social, and economic issues identify and outline the risks and management strategies of a sustainability management system. Installing devices to monitor energy, water consumption, and waste output could enable the hotel to assess and adjust operations for improved sustainability performance. For consistency's sake, the hotel should regularly publish these sustainability reports using frameworks like the Global Reporting Initiative.

While promoting sustainability efforts is crucial for hotels in the eco-conscious travel market, replicating successful communication strategies from one region to another can be tricky. Cultural differences play a significant role, as attitudes towards sustainability vary globally. In some areas, gaining buy-in from staff and guests might require additional effort and resources, including investing in educational programmes to raise awareness and change perceptions. Language barriers can also impede effective communication. If resources are limited, hotels may have to translate materials to reach diverse audiences, which could result in additional costs and potentially limit the reach of their message. Crafting compelling communication materials that resonate with a diverse clientele can also be challenging. Finding a balance between informative and engaging content that appeals to different cultures and languages requires careful consideration and creativity. Successful communication of sustainability efforts requires a nuanced understanding of the local context and a willingness to adapt strategies to meet each region's unique challenges and opportunities.

Infrastructure limitations can pose a significant challenge to replicating successful sustainability models in urban hotels. While renewable energy sources like wind turbines might be feasible in rural areas, urban settings may lack the space or resources for such installations. Additionally, established waste management systems and limited access to local suppliers can hinder efforts to promote eco-friendly practices. However, urban hotels can still adopt several strategies from The Salthouse Hotel's playbook. Retrofitting with energy-efficient LED lighting and motion sensors is a viable option, as is partnering with environmentally conscious waste management companies. These measures reduce the hotel's environmental impact and demonstrate a commitment to sustainability for guests. Navigating regulatory challenges also requires careful consideration. Different regions have varying rules regarding renewable energy, waste management, and other sustainability practices. Balancing compliance with effective communication can be difficult, requiring hotels to understand and adapt to the local regulatory landscape while highlighting their eco-conscious efforts.

Despite these challenges, effective communication of sustainability efforts can lead to increased business, guest loyalty, and positive word-of-mouth referrals. Hotels can use social media, their website, and in-room materials to showcase sustainability initiatives and encourage guests to participate in sustainable practices during their stay. With the right strategies and commitment, hotels can differentiate themselves in the increasingly eco-conscious travel market and reap the benefits of increased business and guest loyalty. It is crucial for hotels to effectively communicate their sustainability efforts to guests while considering the successful communication strategies employed by one hotel.

Conclusion

In conclusion, The Salthouse Hotel's sustainability efforts have resulted in significant environmental, economic, and social benefits for both the hotel and the local community of Ballycastle. However, there is still room for improvement in communication strategies around SDG 11 and overall sustainability. The hotel could improve its communication efforts by making information more accessible, expanding its educational initiatives, communicating more about how it contributes to the local community, emphasising inclusivity and resilience, and sharing more about its sustainability performance. Despite its commendable strides, The Salthouse Hotel has opportunities to enhance its sustainability narrative, particularly about SDG 11. Making metrics more accessible to the public, possibly through an interactive online dashboard, could improve communication. However, all aspects of the hotel's operations, from renewable energy usage to local and eco-friendly purchasing policies, clearly reflect its commitment to sustainability. By effectively communicating its sustainability message and achievements, the hotel promotes a culture of sustainability and encourages guests to adopt eco-friendly practices during their stay. By doing so, the Salthouse Hotel can continue to lead the way in sustainable hospitality and inspire others to follow suit.

Explorations

1. How could The Salthouse Hotel enhance its storytelling techniques and messaging to resonate more effectively with different target audiences?

2. How could it strengthen these relationships to foster a greater sense of community and collective responsibility for sustainable development?

3. Consider information accessibility, language barriers, cultural differences and infrastructure limitations. How could The Salthouse Hotel address these challenges through creative communications strategies?

4. What specific metrics and KPIs could The Salthouse Hotel use to track the impact of its communication on raising awareness, influencing behaviour change, and contributing to SDG 11?

5. While The Salthouse Hotel is in a rural area, what lessons from its sustainability communications strategy could be applied to hotels in urban settings?

XII. Intermezzo 3
Creativity & Storytelling for Effective Communication: Applying Vladimir Propp & Kenneth Burke
Kevin Hora

Introduction

Strategic communications campaigns and practitioners succeed or fail by their use of tactical communications methods. Popular one-size-fits-all tactics, as familiar to practitioners as they are to media, key audiences and the general public, can be effective – press releases, photo ops and social media, for instance. However, while conventional effectiveness may be sufficient for a consumer product launch, or to build support for an uncontentious public information campaign, sustainability campaigns, by dint of the importance advocates and supporters imbue in them, particularly when confronted by opposing audiences that can include the uninformed and uninterested, the misinformed and sceptical, and disinforming agents acting in bad faith, require more considered tactical and strategic insight. This chapter explores the use of creativity and storytelling in public relations. It moves to bridge the dual gaps between theory and practice, and tactics and strategy, and does so by situating creativity and storytelling in contemporary strategic communications practice, identifying instances of excellence in the case studies in this collection.

Creativity is empathetic and strategic, and not merely an end in itself: it takes cognisance of a situation and applies a structured thought process to identify novel ways of engaging with supporting and oppositional publics. However, no matter how tried and tested tactics are, unless they stem from a creative strategy they are limited in their application and what they may achieve. The chapter proposes storytelling as an effective creative process, and identifies in the case studies examples of skilful narrative. In recent years, storytelling has attracted the attention of strategic communications practitioners who see it as a technique that permits effective communication of a point of view through a constructed narrative. There is, however, a difference between having a story to tell, and knowing how to tell it: lack of awareness of this distinction frequently results in clichéd linear narratives of what organisations want to say without having taken proper consideration of audiences and their needs in the process. Vladimir Propp's morphology of the folktale is suggested as a narrative structure that may help practitioners to unlock their strategic creativity as storytellers.

Far from being a one-way conduit of information, good storytelling evokes a response from the intended audience: whether the response is congruent or discordant with the narrative is less important than that the response exists and a dialogue emerges that fosters engagement. In this, it leans towards the rhetorical paradigm of public relations theory, which emphasises the dialogic process of communication, and the potential that the persuader may, in turn, be persuaded by a counter-argument to adjust position. Although Motion *et al.* (2016) suggest that a new paradigm in strategic communications based on "connectivity, engagement and creativity" may be needed, this could be taken to imply that the rhetorical paradigm does not connect, engage or create, yet Kenneth Burke's dramatism, whose foundations are in rhetoric, certainly does. Burke's profoundly consequential thinking, not least as an ecocritical philosopher (Coupe, 2001), naturally lends itself to storytelling: the chapter concludes with an exploration of his dramatism and dramatistic pentad theories and their applicability to strategic communications.

Creativity & Strategic Communications

For an industry that holds creativity with special reverence, surprisingly little of depth has been written on it in academia, while material produced by practitioners tends to fall into the genre of reductive online or magazine-style articles with well-intentioned, but simplistic, advice on how to be more creative. Kent's judgement that "storytelling is treated asymmetrically, as a tool of information dissemination, rather than as a rhetorical strategy that has the power to move people" is apt (Kent, 2015). From an industry perspective, the European Communications Monitor survey of practitioners has engaged very little with creativity in over a decade of reporting, while the Holmes Reports from 2012 onwards tend to look at manifestations or consequences of creativity. For senior executives surveyed by Estanyol & Roca (2015) "creativity still evokes a number of myths and prejudices", not least that it belongs to the advertising or visual communications domains, though they recognise it as a broadly cognitive problem-solving or idea-generating process. Some academics concur, asserting that public relations, not being a creative industry like advertising, must be judged by different criteria or standards (L'Etang, 2008). Popular textbooks frequently list creativity as a desirable attribute of a practitioner, but do not offer deeper insight into what it is (Seitel, 2017; Fawkes, 2012; Fitzpatrick, 2012; Berger & Reber, 2006).

The literature on strategic communications appears to suggest that creativity is something that is tactical rather than strategic. Grunig *et al.* (2002) assert that creativity "generally is associated with the technician role". When respected scholars underplay its strategic importance, it is unsurprising that creativity is considered something merely to be used rather than a potentially transformative aspect of the communications planning process. Against the backdrop of an emerging artificial intelligence future that has the potential to be truly transformative, creativity is still considered tactically as a developing arena, separate to strategy. Thus:

> The ability to develop complex strategies, create creative content and build relationships with clients and media will continue to be critical skills that add value in the PR industry. Skills such as strategic thinking, creativity and interpersonal communication are becoming more important (Seidenglanz & Baier, 2023).

Against this backdrop, any strategic communications activity could claim to be creative on the evidence of a well-crafted press release or eye-catching social media ephemera. However, it is critical skills and interpersonal communication that separate the tactically sound and moderately creative activity from the strategic. *Anyone: Deceived*, a short film created by the Department of Justice and the UN Migration Office in Ireland to drive awareness of human trafficking in Ireland, is a case in point. Sarah-Kate Spratt's study shows how the short drama emotively connects the viewer with the characters, and is targeted at key audiences. Conventional creativity may have elected to produce a factual, documentary style film: the decision to couch the campaign's message in a hard-hitting drama strengthens the audience's response and creates deeper levels of awareness and engagement with a topic that impacts relatively few people in society.

Moriarty (1997) heralded new interest in creativity in public relations, but it proved to be a false dawn with few academics building on his foundations. Moloney is refreshingly provocative with his assertion that, as work, public relations "generates great energy, great commitment, sometimes great creativity" (Moloney, 2000). Here, "sometimes" may be considered more a call to do better as an industry than a negative assessment: when strategic communications is visibly creative, it can produce innovative campaigns that become lodestars for practice. Palea (2010) calls creativity the "essential means for fulfilling objectives in the public relations department" and notes that "success depends on the specialists' capacity to be creative" which extends the definitions into process and application rather than attribute. Green (2007), however, offers a more useful, holistic definition:

> Creativity is the ability each of us has to create something new by bringing together two or more different elements in a new context, in order to provide added value to a task. A creative act consists of not only originating but also evaluating the added value it contributes. It is not novelty for its own sake, but it must produce some form of value that can be recognised by a third party.

This is exemplified by the Grow It Yourself (GIY) movement. Avice Meya's study details the organisation's use of cookery to add value to growing fruit and vegetables. Through a television series, cookery classes at its headquarters, online courses and recipes, GIY creates a tangible outcome for participants that deepens their connection to the seasonality of produce, and stimulates commitment to the organisation's goals.

Green's identification of added value elevates creativity from an attribute or activity carried out as its own orthodoxic end to an essential element of strategic communications. Heterodoxic thinking may be a useful perspective, particularly for organisations, like many detailed in this book operating from a civic society background, to compete on a more equal footing with orthodoxic corporate interests:

> The main targets for many campaigns, for example, are multinational corporations, so there are clear differences in availability of economic resources between the targets and those who are targeting them; but, by using the logic of the mass media (for example, the David against Goliath syndrome), these differences can be less significant than might be supposed. Here one could also see how the use of creativity and unconventional ideas could bring advantages to networks (Fredriksson, 2009).

The visual representation of Coalition Against Hate Crime Ireland's *Hate Crime Hurts Us All* campaign replaces the Goliath of corporate adversity with that of society at large. What could have been a workmanlike communications campaign of social media and advertising images depicting real people who had been subjected to abuse was elevated by transforming the campaign launch into an art exhibition, held in a prestigious gallery. The transformation of the image from cause-related publicity to art chimes with Berger's treatise on the ephemeral nature of the publicity image as a staging point between the past and the desirable future. Such images "belong to the moment in the sense that they must be continually renewed and made up-to-date. Yet they never speak of the present. Often, they refer to the past and always they speak of the future" (Berger, 1972). In this instance, a repressive past found its repudiation in an emotionally honest, optimistic future. The art gallery, a cultural space denoting civilised society, became both the host to and domain of the David-like coalition of minority advocacy groups, momentarily finding their expression in their shared belonging in Irish society.

Storytelling & Propp's Morphology of the Folktale

These examples told their stories creatively. Like creativity, storytelling has no shortage of advocates in strategic communications, and has witnessed an increase in academic attention in the last decade (Coombs & Holladay, 2018). Kent (2015) notes that "tens of thousands of professionals now offer advice online for using stories in public relations". Storytelling has the attraction of being simple to understand and easy to use at a tactical level, as it has been intrinsic to human existence from the earliest cave drawings to modern digital storytelling (Özoran & Üzümlü, 2024). Ostensibly it is easy to define, being simply the transmission of a narrative from one person to another with the intent to inform or entertain. Other forms of storytelling may have a moralistic or didactic purpose, as, for example, fairy tales. Such definitions are of limited value to strategic communications but are the approaches most likely taken by practitioners possessing an incomplete understanding of the potential of storytelling. Lee *et al.*'s (2016) comprehensive definition is instructive in such cases:

> Storytelling includes the elements of concept, character, theme, structure, and voice, and all of which are transmitted through oral, pictorial, written, or film media forms. The purpose of storytelling is not only to describe a situation but also to motivate people to act in a certain way.

Nonetheless, it focuses on the process and desired result of storytelling. Gill's (2015) examination of corporate storytelling from a corporate social responsibility perspective holds that it is a narrative act with the potential to capture the imagination and attention of audiences that presents incidents and actions of the storyteller in a way that rises above gender, ethnicity, culture and age. While van den Broek (2021) cautions that narrative fidelity is not always evident in corporate communications where greenwashing narratives are selectively chosen by organisations to manage perception of their activities and reputation, a socially acceptable narrative is one where consistency between the past and future is evident. The same cautionary approach applies to NGO and advocacy storytelling, where a virtuous agenda can be let down by narrative inconsistencies between what is told and done.

Jørgen *et al.* (2021) hold that storytelling is an experientially transformative process concerned with our appearance before an audience, which establishes the uniqueness of our identity, and our agency to speak. This further identifies us as belonging to the same community as our audience, while the public nature of our storytelling renders it a political act. Storytelling, thus, becomes integral to the public good. Brown (2020) takes a similar view, noting that environmental interests have increasingly understood "the importance of storytelling to change people's hearts, minds, and behaviours, rebooting a fatalistic narrative to one of hope and action". The language of the story becomes critical in this space, as it creates communal accord between the teller and audience, the participants, while identifying oppositional voices.

This leads to the importance of creating meaning in storytelling. A narrative offered only to further the ends of the storyteller becomes a non-discursive act where acquiescence is the only acceptable outcome for the teller. It is the role of the strategic communications practitioner to create storytelling modes that enable public discourse and stimulate responses. Receivers of the story become participants, but only if they believe the stories and ensuing dialogues are meaningful and worthy of their engagement (Motion *et al.*, 2016). Stories with meaning are invaluable to organisations communicating complex ideas like sustainability matters as they help to distinguish between the corporate speak that typifies much traditional public relations output and the constructive, dialogic communication that evokes an audience response (Gill, 2015).

Lee *et al.* (2016) observe that Western thinking is based on "logical deductive reasoning" whereas non-Western thinking uses "oral tradition, narratives, and storytelling as primary means to help people understand and make sense". Neuroscience, according to Moreno (2020), also offers evidence that, rather than argumentatively, people think narratively. Ireland has a folkloric tradition that, although diminishing as global multimedia unseats oral heritage, nonetheless spans centuries from the medieval Bardic tradition to remain within living memory. It is not fallacious to suggest that a national culture formed by storytelling should be amenable to it in public discourse, especially when a folkloric interpretative framework, Propp's morphology of the folktale, exists to analyse stories.

Published in 1928, Vladimir Propp's study of Russian folktales systematised their narrative structure by examining functions of narrative elements, rather than their themes or socially didactic purpose. Unknown in anglophone academia for three decades, and notwithstanding the cultural specificity of its origins, it has subsequently proven useful in examining contemporary literature and media (Dogra, 2017). Its usefulness to strategic communications has not been widely explored, yet it is a theory that can sit comfortably within both the systems theory and rhetorical paradigms of public relations. Propp (1968) wrote that:

'Morphology' means the study of forms. In botany, the term 'morphology' means the study of the component parts of a plant, of their relationship to each other and to the whole – in other words, the study of a plant's structure.

This biological explanation aligns it with the systems approach that emphasises structural connectedness and the interdependencies of the organisation and internal and external audiences. As L'Etang (2008) explains:

The systems metaphor sees the world as living, interacting organisms. It is a holistic approach which can be seen to provide an understanding of any set of relationships or domains. … Systems theory emerged in academic thinking in the late 1960s and early 1970s and came from a number of different areas such physics, information theory, biology, communications and media studies.

Pieczka's overview of equilibrium, homeostasis, adaptive and autopoiesis variations within systems theory embrace the principles underpinning Propp's morphology (Pieczka, 1996). It also marries with the rhetorical paradigm, beyond the obvious dialogic relationship. Ihlen (2011), stating that the "rhetorical theory of public relations focuses on the symbolic and relationship building aspects that organisations engage in", links it to Bitzer's notion of the rhetorical situation, a complex melange of actors, relationships and settings, that requires rhetorical discourse for resolution. The rhetorical situation consists of a pressing problem, the audience, and constraints, and these are approachable in an application of Propp's theory.

It is impossible, in so short a space, to interrogate and apply Propp's morphology in its entirety. It comprises two essential elements: functions and characters. Propp isolated 31 functions that always occur sequentially. Dogra (2017) delineates all 31, and notes that the function of characters is always stable: each character is defined by their role; the number of functions is limited and always sequentially identical, though not every story will contain all 31 functions; and all stories are structurally the same. For the communications practitioner, the narrative flow from the first function, absentation (the hero leaves home and the quest begins), to the last, wedding (the hero marries and takes the throne), offers a crib sheet in creativity that allows identification of the desired story, pitfalls, and villains en route to the resolution. This is a far superior approach to merely telling a tale that the organisation or client wishes to be known. A cautionary interjection would recognise that such strict sequentialism favours the primacy of the system and its interdependencies of characters and actions over the human element, which, outside the pages of a fairy tale, can be emotional and irrational; a similar argument can be made of the systems theory paradigm.

Of more immediate use to the storytelling communicator is Propp's *dramatis personae* of seven typical characters common to folktales. He observed that each is, properly, a sphere of action rather than a figure. The spheres are:

- **Hero**: The main figure who embarks on a quest, suffering tribulations until achieving success;
- **Villain**: The character who opposes or tries to thwart the hero;
- **Donor**: The character who give the hero with a magical agent or help in the quest;
- **Helper**: The character who supports the hero with tangible aid or companionship;
- **Princess (and her father)**: A metaphor for the reward for the hero's efforts, often portrayed as a damsel in distress. The father, often hostile to prospective suitors, may set the hero additional tasks to prove himself worthy of the princess;
- **Dispatcher**: The character who sets the hero on the quest;
- **False Hero**: The character who appears to be a hero but is ultimately a fraud or rival to the hero (Propp, 1968).

The spheres offer a valuable framework for analysing the roles and functions of characters in any strategic communications campaign. Joy *et al.* (2023) provide an illuminating assessment of LVMH's social and environmental responsibility reporting by applying them: the CEO, leading the quest, is the hero; the UN, the donor, with its enabling gift of the SDGs that will allow the villain, climate change, to be defeated. Morrell & Tuck applied the same lens to taxation in Britain. Taking "a strong, rather than literal reading" they found characters' identity was fluid rather than fixed, and depended on the perspective of the players. One permutation pitted multinational corporations seeking to minimise their liability as the villain, against HMRC or the Revenue Commissioners, and the hero whose quest is to increase returns for better public services, the princess. In another, HMRC was the villain from the ordinary taxpayer and corporate perspective over perceived heavy handedness in applying rules (Morrell & Tuck, 2014).

Jade Marron's delineation of Leave No Trace Ireland's *Love This Place* campaign likewise lends itself to this deconstruction. The hero is the organisation itself, whose quest is to reduce littering in scenic locations; its tribulations are people spoiling the environment. The villain is those responsible through negligence or ignorance for making the countryside less enjoyable for others. Leave No Trace Ireland identified several villains, but each is recognisable by their actions that thwart the hero's actions. The despatcher is the coalition of organisations that initiated Leave No Trace Ireland's quest for the princess – a clean environment for communal social use. Her father, however, sets new challenges for the hero: to the initial challenge of combating littering was added dog fouling, single use barbecues and dangerous campfires. Rozanna Purcell was the donor. Her social media presence and reach to 170,000 followers was a magical aid to the hero. The helper was the public who adhered to the campaign's messages or participated in public events – the dog-friendly hike and litter-picking for example – while the false hero was members of the public who engaged on social media but not in the countryside itself. What becomes clear with any application of Propp's morpheme is that, with strategic planning, every target audience can be identified as a character. This further discloses their role and motivations so that the morphological structure itself unlocks the practitioner's storytelling capabilities.

Storytelling & Kenneth Burke's Dramatism Theory

While Propp's work was gaining traction in Russia, coincidentally in America the literary critic Kenneth Burke began to formulate dramatism theory. Originating in the 1930s, his theory, a way of probing the texts he critiqued, was gaining a disparate academic audience outside literary and dramatic circles, even "lurking in sociologists' footnotes" as one commentator expresses it (Overington, 1977). Accelerating with World War II, Burke expanded its application to other discourses, including news media and social discourse, with the publication of the seminal *A Grammar of Motives* in 1945, in which he analysed the motivations for human communication as a form of action (Weiser, 2007). Burke (1968a) wrote that dramatism is:

> A method of analysis and corresponding critique of terminology as designed to show that the most direct route to the study of human relations and human motives is via a methodical inquiry into the cycles or clusters of terms and their functions.

Such thinking led rhetorical public relations scholars to reify his theories in practice (*inter alia*, Ihlen, 2011; Brown, 2015; Heath, 2009).

Rather than an analysis of methods of conveying information, dramatism is a lens for analysing relationships through language and its consequences, with three particular facets. First, all life is drama. There is a vogue in strategic communications to emphasise storytelling as a panacea, but frequently the stories told lack vitality or impose an implausible ending that plays on publics' credulousness. What ersatz storytelling overlooks is that at the heart of all drama lies conflict. This may be the gap between what an organisation says and what publics hear: the denouement of the drama is reconciliation of the parties, akin to the win-win zone in the Grunigian paradigm's two-way symmetrical communication (Grunig *et al.*, 2002).

Second, Burke insisted that the author not only reported the meaning of their words, but conveyed their emotional impact so recipients experienced the same emotional response the author had in creating them (Heath, 2013). Third, people play roles where they are motivated to act responsively within their stage-setting. Burke suggested guilt guided emotions and motivations, and that communication choices are influenced by a desire to relieve guilt (Burke, 1945). Communications practitioners must be aware that individuals are actors with their own agency, motivated to act in certain ways when they experience drama in their social, political and cultural spheres. Intrinsic in Burkeanism is that motivation is not the pure persuasion of most rhetorical thinking, but the identification of the communicator with the audience; of finding common ground in the use of language and symbols that leads to cooperation (Hochmuth, 1952). Engaging persuasively with rational sceptics fails to grasp that their dialogue, far from being performative, is their expression of agency relative to their peers. Understanding dramatic storytelling becomes critically important, therefore, in identifying with audiences, and especially in sustainability issues where rational and irrational contestability are evident.

Inspired by a photographic exhibition where the photographer, using different coloured filters, created different representations of the same subject, Burke originated terministic screens, which explain how we perceive and symbolically respond to the world around us (Heath, 2013), and how symbols can direct attention in one direction rather another (Stob, 2008). Burke (1968b) defined scientific and dramatistic screens:

The 'scientistic' approach builds the edifice of language with primary stress upon a proposition such as "it is, or it is not". The 'dramatistic' approach puts the primary stress upon such hortatory expressions as "thou shalt", or "thou shalt not".

The nuance is in the shift from the indicative mood, stating fact, to the imperative mood, conveying instruction. Put simply, the scientific screen defines a term unambiguously, as strategic communications professionals might strive for accuracy and truth in fact. The dramatistic screen concerns action, and how the recipient's interpretation of the message persuades or motivates them to act. Communicating through the scientific screen without considering the dramatistic risks ineffective communication as publics have interpretative options that motivate their response. They can ask what object in reality does the term reflect? What qualities does the term emphasise? What qualities does it deflect or conceal, that is, where are the opposite interpretations? What other terms relate to it, and how?

Good storytelling anticipates these questions, and Burke's dramatistic pentad, which loosely corresponds to the Five Ws of news writing, offers a framework that is as strategic as it is creative. The five points of the pentad are the act, scene, agent, agency and purpose. The act is associated with the event, past or current, in thought or deed. The scene is the locus of the event and where and when it took place. It includes context and background material. The agent is the actor who carries out the action. Agency is the 'how' element: how did the agent act, and what instrument did they use? The purpose addresses why; it is linked to the actor's motivation which comes from interpretation through a terministic screen. Used retrospectively, the pentad identifies where and why communication took place but it can also be used predictively in planning.

Burke proposed 10 possible perspectives in the pentad, with each perspective combining two elements into a ratio to examine shifting points of view. These are scene combined with act, agent, agency, and purpose; act combined with purpose, agent and agency; agent combined with purpose and agency; and agency-purpose (Burke, 1945, p.15). It is possible to determine the communicator's perspective from the first word in each ratio. If communication stems from the act, it is underscored by realism, and active language is to the fore. Materialism, that is, the material setting, stems from scene-led ratios. For agent-led ratios, focusing on the human or interpersonal connectedness, the ideology is idealism. Agency, because of its role in how an action is achieved, suggests a measure of pragmatism, while purpose, rendering the individual, or organisation, second to the outcome, has its compulsion in mysticism (German, 2009).

Burke specifically treated the agent-act and scene-agent ratios to explain his theory (Burke, 1945): when strategic communications motivate an individual to act as desired, that is agent-act. Where the locus of the communication motivates an individual is the scene-agent ratio. If Burke intended that drama is a form of analysis of action, then "drama 'works' only when it draws on these cultural expectations so as to build plot and characters around these ratios" (Overington, 1977). Applying Burke's ratios predictively to a campaign can facilitate the strategist in harnessing the storytelling capability of the terministic screen and the dramatistic pentad to determine audiences, their motivations and the consequences of their actions. Thus, each ratio used in planning becomes a terministic screen, altering the communications strategist's perspective of angles to approach the campaign from, while the desired outcome remains, in essence, the same.

The WorkEqual campaign, for instance, provides scope for analysis using multiple ratios. Applying the scene-agent ratio, the locus of the action is the work environment in which women are treated unequally. The agent, motivated by the setting, is the WorkEqual organisation itself. In the scene-act ratio, the scene remains the same while the act is the *Equal Pay Day*, seminars and events the organisation organises to draw attention to the inequality. Burke's thinking is consistent with many public relations theories. In agent-purpose, WorkEqual is compelled to exist to address the goal of ending gender employment inequality – this is redolent of the public relations maxim that issues create publics, or serve to identify "emergent groupings involved in making an issue of something that is publicly contested" (Amelung & Machado, 2019). The scene-purpose ratio – the workplace environment and society being the place where the inequality exists – is the motivation to demonstrate an expression of purpose: in this, parallels may be drawn with Habermassian public sphere theory with its emphasis on rights-based conditions for open discourse with the purpose of influencing political institutions' decision making (Dryzek *et al.*, 2006).

Conclusion

Far from being the preserve of a talented few, creativity and storytelling in strategic communications are skills that can be developed by all practitioners. The structures offered by Propp and Burke, both theorists at home within strategic communication's rhetorical and systems theory paradigms, give practitioners the cognitive advantage to strategise what they need to say, to whom, and how best to couch it in terms that will resonate with audiences. Effective storytelling enables the teller to consider their narrative from different character viewpoints and axes of perspective, and to create compelling stories that are authentic, meaningful and identify not only with the audience's beliefs, but their misconceptions and hostilities also. For organisations engaged in communicating and advocating the sustainability goals themselves or campaigns to give effect to them, storytelling can simplify complex ideas in a vernacular language, frame unwelcome news or interdictions as a stage in a journey, and give each member of the audience their participatory agency. This chapter suggests that moving storytelling from a basic tactical mode of imparting information to a strategic mode is better for both the teller and the audience, two different elements, harkening to Green's definition, brought together in a new context that adds recognisable value to the creative, communicative act.

References

Amelung, N. & Machado, H. (2019). Affected for good or for evil: The formation of issue-publics that relate to the UK National DNA Database. *Public Understanding of Science*, 28(5), pp.590–605.

Berger, J. (1972). *Ways of Seeing*. London: BBC/Penguin.

Berger, B.K. & Reber, B.H. (2006). *Gaining Influence in Public Relations: The Role of Resistance in Practice*. Mahwah, NJ: Lawrence Erlbaum Associates.

Brown, R.E. (2015). *The Public Relations of Everything: The Ancient, Modern & Postmodern Dramatic History of an Idea*. Abingdon, Oxon: Routledge.

Brown, T. (2020). Science, Storytelling, and Students: The National Geographic Society's On Campus Initiative. In: S. Mickey, M.E. Tucker & J. Grim (eds.). *Living Earth Community: Multiple Ways of Being & Knowing*. Cambridge: Open Book Publisher.

Burke, K. (1945). *A Grammar of Motives*. New York: Prentice-Hall.

Burke, K. (1968a). Dramatism. In: D.L. Sills (ed.). *International Encyclopedia of the Social Sciences*. New York: Macmillan Publishing Company.

Burke, K. (1968b). *Language as Symbolic Action. Essays on Life, Literature & Method*. Oaklands, CA: University of California Press.

Coombs, W.T. & Holladay, S.J. (2018). Innovation in public relations theory and practice: A transmedia narrative transportation (TNT) approach. *Journal of Communication Management*, Volume 22, pp.382-396.

Coupe, L. (2001). Kenneth Burke: Pioneer of ecocriticism. *Journal of American Studies*, 35(3), pp.413–31.

Dogra, S. (2017). The 31 functions in Vladimir Propp's morphology of the folktale: An outline and recent trends in the applicability of the Proppian taxonomic model. *Rupkatha Journal on Interdisciplinary Studies in Humanities, ix(2)*, pp.410-19.

Dryzek, J.S., Honig, B. & Phillips, A. (2006). Introduction. In: *The Oxford Handbook of Political Theory*. Oxford: Oxford University Press.

Estanyol, E. & Roca, D. (2015). Creativity in PR consultancies: Perception and management. *Public Relations Review*, 41, pp.589–597.

Fawkes, J. (2012). What is Public Relations? In: A. Theaker (ed.). *The Handbook of Public Relations*. Abingdon, Oxon: Routledge.

FitzPatrick, L. (2012). Internal Communications. In: A. Theaker (ed.). *The Handbook of Public Relations*. Abingdon, Oxon: Routledge.

Fredriksson, M. (2009). On Beck: Risk & Subpolitics in Reflexive Modernity. In: Ø. Ihlen, B. van Ruler & M. Fredriksson (eds.). *Public Relations & Social Theory: Key Figures & Concepts*. Abingdon, Oxon: Routledge

German, K.M. (2009). Dramatism & Dramatistic Pentad. In: S.W. Littlejohn & K.A. Foss (eds.). *Encyclopedia of Communication Theory*. London: Sage.

Gill, R. (2015). Why the PR strategy of storytelling improves employee engagement and adds value to CSR: An integrated literature review. *Public Relations Review*, 41, pp.662–674.

Green, A. (2007). *Creativity in Public Relations*. 2 ed. London: Kogan Page.

Grunig, L.A., Grunig, J.E. & Dozier, D. (2002). *Excellent Public Relations & Effective Organisations. A Study of Communication Management in Three Countries*. Mahwah, NJ: Lawrence Erlbaum Associates.

Heath, R.L. (2009). The Rhetorical Tradition: Wrangle in the Marketplace. In: R.L. Heath, E.L. Toth & D. Waymer (eds.). *Rhetorical & Critical Approaches to Public Relations*. New York: Routledge.

Heath, R.L. (2013). Dramatism & Dramatism Theory. In: R.L. Heath (ed.). *Encyclopedia of Public Relations*. 2 ed. Thousand Oaks, Ca: Sage.

Hochmuth, M. (1952). Kenneth Burke and the 'New Rhetoric'. *Quarterly Journal of Speech*, 38(2), pp.133–44.

Ihlen, Ø. (2011). On barnyard scrambles: Toward a rhetoric of public relations. *Management Communication Quarterly*, 25(3), pp.455– 473.

Jørgen, K.M., Strand, A.M.C., Hayden, J., Spaare, M. & Larsen, J. (2021). Down to earth: Gaia storytelling and the learning organization. *The Learning Organization*, 28(5), pp.464-477.

Joy, A., Roberts, J., Grohmann, B. & Peña, C. (2023). Confronting climate crisis through corporate narratives: The fairy tale in LVMH's 2020 and 2021 social and environmental responsibility reports. *Luxury*, 10(1-2), pp.81–118.

Kent, M.L. (2015). The power of storytelling in public relations: Introducing the 20 master plots. *Public Relations Review*, Volume 41, pp.480–489.

Lee, H., Fawcett, J. & DeMarco, R.R. (2016). Storytelling / narrative theory to address health communication with minority populations. *Applied Nursing Research*, 30, pp.58-60.

L'Etang, J. (2008). *Public Relations Concepts, Practice & Critique*. London: Sage.

Moloney, K. (2000). *Rethinking Public Relations: The Spin & the Substance*. 1 ed. Abingdon, Oxon: Routledge.

Moreno, L.D.R. (2020). Sustainable city storytelling: Cultural heritage as a resource for a greener and fairer urban development. *Journal of Cultural Heritage Management & Sustainable Development*, 10(4), pp.399-412.

Moriarty, S.E. (1997). The Big Idea: Creativity in Public Relations. In: C.L. Caywood (ed.). *The Handbook of Strategic Public Relations & Integrated Communications*. Boston, MA: McGraw Hill.

Morrell, K. & Tuck, P. (2014). Governance, tax and folk tales. *Accounting, Organizations & Society*, 39, pp.134–147.

Motion, J., Heath, R.L. & Leitch, S. (2016). *Social Media & Public Relations. Fake Friends & Powerful Publics*. Abingdon, Oxon: Routledge.

Overington, M.A. (1977). Kenneth Burke and the method of dramatism. *Theory & Society*, 14(1), pp.131-156.

Özoran, B.A. & Üzümlü, A.M. (2024). Storytelling as a tool for activist public relations: A qualitative study in case of women. *Selçuk Üniversitesi Sosyal Bilimler Enstitüsü Dergisi*, 53, pp.352-366.

Palea, A. (2010). Creativity in public relations. *Professional Communication & Translation Studies*, 3(1-2), pp.19-24.

Pieczka, M. (1996). Paradigms, Systems Theory & Public Relations. In: J. L'Etang (ed.). *Critical Perspectives in Public Relations*. London: International Thomson Business Press.

Propp, V. (1968). *Morphology of the Folktale*. 2 ed. Revised and Edited with a *Preface* by Louis A. Wagner and New Introduction by Alan Dundes. Austin: University of Texas Press.

Seidenglanz, R. & Baier, M. (2023). The Impact of Artificial Intelligence on the Professional Field of Public Relations/Communications Management: Ethical Issues, Challenges & an Attempt at a Forecast. In: A. Adi (ed.), *Artificial Intelligence in Public Relations Communications*. Berlin: Quadriga UInivesity of Applied Sciences.

Seitel, F.P. (2017). *The Practice of Public Relations*. 13 ed. Harlow, Essex: Pearson.

Stob, P. (2008). 'Terministic screens', social constructionism, and the language of experience: Kenneth Burke's utilization of William James. *Philosophy & Rhetoric*, 41(2), pp.130-52.

van den Broek, O. (2021). Narrative fidelity: Making the UN Sustainable Development Goals fit. *Corporate Communications: An International Journal*, 26(3), pp.441-460.

Weiser, M.E. (2007). Burke and war: Rhetoricizing the theory of dramatism. *Rhetoric Review*, 26(3), pp.286-302.

XIII. SDG 13 – Climate Action
Friends of the Earth's *Cuppa for Climate* Campaign

Martha O'Brien

Abstract

The Friends of the Earth's *Cuppa for Climate* campaign goal was to create a conversation about the impact of climate change and how everybody can be involved in helping. This campaign relied on people hosting events and using the organisation's toolkit and guide in order to talk about the environment and environmental issues over a social cup of tea. This is a popular tactic in Ireland. However, as the case study shows, it did not lend itself naturally to the environmental sphere, with the result that the campaign achieved only modest results for Friends of the Earth. What makes this campaign valuable from a communications perspective is that Friends of the Earth showed adaptability and initiative in refocusing a campaign that did not achieve its desired outcomes.

Introduction

The fight to the save the environment is long and challenging. Businesses have attempted to reduce their eco footprint for socially responsible and business reasons, while non-profit and charitable organisations do so with the goal of helping the environment. Among the latter is the non-profit organisation Friends of the Earth, which initiated the *Cuppa for Climate* campaign to address SDG 13 – Climate Action. Much of the environmental damage has been manmade, and what is not manmade has been made worse by mankind. This SDG is about stopping climate change, pollution, global warming and other ecological damage. This is one of the greatest and most important challenges on earth at this moment and so this SDG is of foremost importance for the world. Ruth Jedidja Stael, Support Care Officer of Friends of the Earth, explained the relevance of this SDG to the organisation: "By adopting sustainable practices, reducing carbon emissions, and conserving natural habitats, we can mitigate the adverse effects of human activities on the planet".

Friends of the Earth identified a key problem that needed to be addressed to build the movement's power to bring about system change and ensure no-one is left behind: a lack of place to talk about environmental issues. The campaign has unusual origins. It came about after a comedy show by Irish comedian Colm O'Regan, in which he made jokes about the environment, that was followed by a guest talk. Attendees gave feedback on how much they enjoyed having a space to talk about climate issues and how hard it can be to start a conversation on the topic with other people.

Background

One of the main organisational challenges for Friends of the Earth is how to stay in the public eye while it carries out multiple campaigns that may evolve over a lengthy period of time with few milestone achievements to maintain public interest. The discourse surrounding climate change can be challenging, with climate denial and hostility dissuading many ordinary people from participating. While many of its campaigns take a long time to achieve tangible results, the distinctive appeal of the *Cuppa for Climate* campaign was that, as a variation of the popular coffee-morning tactic, it was about setting smaller goals, with most of the work to host the events, and generate awareness of the issue, being done by the public. The goals of the campaign were to bring attention to climate action, get people involved in action to help and to raise awareness of Friends of the Earth and its work. While many of the events included raising money for Friends of the Earth, this was not a goal of the campaign but a welcome side effect.

While conventional public relations wisdom suggests that publics need to be clearly identified for messaging to be effective, the primary communications goal for this campaign was to bring a wide range of people from all walks of life together to connect around climate and get started on taking communal positive action. The campaign cost the Friends of the Earth very little, but it brought attention to the organisation, and allowed people to get involved in ways to help the planet at local level where informality and personal networks can be highly effective at stimulating conversation about the environment. The strategy of the campaign was to get people to host their own events, using supplies from Friends of the Earth. The organisation supplied a toolkit for hosts and guests sharing a *Cuppa for Climate*. The toolkit was about climate action and all events were about bringing attention to, and helping fight, climate change. This allowed people to host the events in the way they wanted and the way that suited them, so while the events may have differed in size, activities were all about raising awareness and getting people involved.

Tactics & Activities

Friends of the Earth observed that there was a large number of people who wanted to do something about climate change but did not know where to start. The *Cuppa for Climate* was a friendly introduction to the topic of environmentalism and climate change. The main tactic Friends of the Earth employed for the *Cuppa for Climate* campaign was spreading word of the campaign using social media. The main platforms Friends of the Earth uses are X and Instagram, while there is a video made by the organisation on YouTube and Instagram talking about and promoting the campaign. However, given the type of campaign, the primary focus was on Instagram where hashtags and the visual appeal of photographs and images would influence other groups to post about their *Cuppa for Climate* events.

Using a hashtag allowed people a chance to get involved in a way that suited their needs at the time and, because the coffee mornings were hosted by the individual, it allowed for the commitment level to suit the consumer. It also allowed people who were hosting events to link the event and for Friends of the Earth to acknowledge it. Properly promoted, this made social media a self-sustaining communications tactic: people would see the hashtag, the pictures, and the cause on Instagram and be motivated to host their own *Cuppa for Climate* event. In turn, more people would host events, posting on their social media accounts, thereby causing more people to know about the cause, which in turn would lead to more events. This viral effect is both cost-effective and pervasive.

However, just as pathogenic viruses mutate, so too can viral communications. The self-sustaining aspect of the communications campaign was important to keeping momentum going on the engagement, but it raised the potential issue of non-regulated events in Friends of the Earth's name, especially those with a fundraising activity. While Friends of the Earth made it clear that *Cuppa for Climate* events did not have to be fundraisers for their charity, an event hosted that contain information that was misaligned with the campaign's goals could have been damaging to its brand image and reputation. *Cuppa for Climate* required a potential host of an event to apply to host it. Hosts were provided with a toolkit for the event to make sure the information they disseminated was correct. The toolkit contained helpful advice on organising events from small gatherings of family and friends to larger get-togethers and prompts for questions and conversations that hosts could use to get a dialogue going.

To formally launch the campaign, Friends of the Earth partnered with Bewley's Coffee Shop on Dublin's Grafton Street, an historic landmark and part of the city's social and cultural fabric, in April 2023. The launch coincided with *Earth Day 2023* (April 22) and marked the 49th anniversary of Friends of the Earth in Ireland. Billed as a community-building initiative, the launch featured a discussion panel chaired by the organisation's CEO, Oisín Coghlan, and several environmental guest speakers. These included Molly O'Shea, a member of Young Friends of the Earth and the Friends of the Earth board, Sarah O'Suilleabhain, a member of One Future and the Friends of the Earth board, and Carol-Anne O'Brien, co-founder of BOLD Climate Action, a group that facilitates participation by older people in climate action awareness.

Results & Outcomes

Their venture seemed set for success, as the launch in Bewley's Café received limited coverage in the national and local media. Achieving newspaper coverage for an event that, while professionally organised and in a well-known location, was not entirely noteworthy and competing with other interests for coverage, was a good start. However, momentum did not build as anticipated. Despite several Friends of the Earth press releases in the weeks leading up to the launch, it did not receive significant coverage. Earned media channels are highly competitive and the news story did not stand out sufficiently to receive extensive coverage.

Owned channels should have been more forthcoming, but even these did not generate momentum, or generate high numbers of reposts or drive dialogue. Research in December 2023 indicated that there were just four tweets on X using the hashtag #CuppaforClimate that were not from Friends of the Earth. X, of course was not a focal point of the social media campaign, which may explain the low number of posts, and there is no indication of the number of posts there of people's own parties that they hosted without using the hashtag. There were 15 posts on Instagram about *Cuppa for Climate*. Again, there is no straightforward way to tell if there were more posts that did not use the hashtags but put the event name in the description. While likes are an unreliable indicator of public engagement, most of the posts had low to medium double-digit likes. Comments on the posts were negligible.

By the end of 2023, 15 known events had been hosted, about two per month since the April launch. Friends of the Earth did receive more applications for the toolkits than there were known events hosted. However, it is unclear how many of those applications translated into actual events that were organised without notifying Friends of the Earth or using the hashtag or were events that were planned that had not taken place by the end of 2023. The lack of information is disappointing, as these events had potential to attract a mix of already committed activists, new participants and even policymakers. Friends of the Earth's Instagram feed contains a video of one such event in Inchicore, Dublin, organised by a recent arrival to the area and a colleague as a very informal opportunity to meet likeminded people. Among those who participated were two elected public representatives from the Green Party and Sinn Féin, which gives an indication of the type of public pressure the campaign could have generated.

Critical Analysis

Friends of the Earth's *Cuppa for Climate* campaign was not the success it should have been. This is partly because there were no clear results that can be measured from this campaign, as there was no direct goal to achieve. Creating a dialogue around climate change is necessary and worthwhile but without being linked to a tangible activity like fundraising, as most similar activities are, or as part of a campaign to put public pressure on policymakers, it lacked a meaningful focus that would attract people who were only somewhat interested in the climate crisis. This campaign was simple in concept, which should have contributed to making it easy for audiences to adopt, but it was not as well executed as it could have been. While there was no goal to achieve other than promoting climate awareness, and even fund-raising – usually a priority for hard-pressed activist organisations – was discretionary, it is hard to say there was a total failure to the campaign as it achieved some limited success.

The biggest flaw was in the social media campaign. This campaign could have been entirely self-sufficient, using social media viral effect and word of mouth to reach audiences. When people hosted the event, they should have been required to hashtag *#CuppaforClimate* and tag Friends of the Earth. People who followed someone who hosted the event, and were interested themselves could hit the hashtag, they would see others hosting the events and the video would be there telling them what to do. That was not done and most groups who hosted did not link or hashtag: anyone who would be interested would have found it hard to get information as the posts were not always clear. This lost the campaign a lot of traction for growth of the campaign.

When looking at the campaign, there is a lack of engagement on X and TikTok. While X is an increasingly controversial platform for what appears to be light-handed moderation of content that gives climate-denial views some prominence, TikTok, for its reach with younger audiences and short video-friendly content, can reach outside of the average audience of Friends of the Earth. TikTok could have been a great tool for this campaign. Its algorithm could have allowed for just one well-promoted event to go viral. While Instagram was a sensible platform to use for this campaign, one more social media platform could have expanded the reach more effectively. The lesson in this is to consider where audiences can most easily be found and communicated with.

Coffee mornings are a very popular tactic for bringing people together to promote issues and concerns in Ireland. It was a sensible activity for Friends of the Earth to engage in. However, most similar events are connected to issues like health and mental health issues, which affect most people personally or though knowing somebody affected. This makes them very naturally occurring conversations. There is also something to consider that forcing a conversation is not as effective as believed. The Irish are known for being able to talk about everything, but it rare to talk about environmental issues. These are not a natural conversation starters when groups meet for coffee mornings, the way with other topics are. The main themes for the cuppa events were talking about climate problems, what people can do about climate change, and how to fix the problems. While the tool kit gave pointers for creating an environment to have the climate conversation, this meant that environment was artificially created, which made it feel less authentic and spontaneous. It would have helped Friends of the Earth if the conversations could have been done from a more personal, local level to achieve authenticity.

One campaign with limited success cannot take from the fact that Friends of the Earth has had many successful campaigns and, over the course of half a century, has achieved a lot as an advocacy organisation. Its *Power to the People* campaign, for example, which was about bringing solar energy to schools demonstrates this: all schools use energy and changing the source of power in those schools is important to lower the use of fossil fuel. This led to a highly successful campaign that led to the implementation of Schools Photovoltaic Programme. Most case studies in any collection examine organisations that have had near-perfect campaigns, but a good measure of strategic communications practice is what happens when campaigns do not go to plan. Adaptability and flexibility are crucial in strategic communications as they allow organisations to recognise when a campaign is not realising its aims, and to take corrective action.

Since the campaign began, Friends of the Earth have evaluated it and now plan to join it with another campaign, *Act Local*, to maximise the effectiveness of both campaigns. This shows great strategic understanding from Friends of the Earth and demonstrates sound judgement. Instead of shutting down *Cuppa for Climate* when it did not deliver expected results, the organisation re-evaluated the campaign to assess the problems, recognised that the campaign still offered potential and would work better as a tool in a much larger campaign than on its own. Combining with *Act Local* makes sense, as it creates the definitive association with tangible goals that *Cuppa for Climate* lacked.

Act Local is an existing Friends of the Earth campaign. It has two main focuses: Space for Nature and Connected Communities. This campaign's tactics are the same as *Cuppa for Climate* in that Friends of the Earth communicate online *via* social media campaigns. Space for Nature is about protecting animals and nature. There has been a decline in the number of animals on the planet and rise in the number of extinct animals. This campaign is about saving the environments these animals need and restoring what can be restored to give them a place to live. It is also concerned with removing invasive species of plants that are taking over areas and threatening native species and precious ecosystems. Connected Communities is about vehicles. The damage that larger vehicles like SUVs, and even lighter cars due to their sheer numbers on the roads, cause to the environment cannot be downplayed. To limit the damage that these vehicles do, the goal of this campaign is to create a bicycle focus in communities as their preferred mode of transportation. It takes its inspiration from The Netherlands which made its cities bicycle-friendly by creating infrastructure that facilitated it. This structure could be translated into an Irish city with government assistance. Having combined the two, Friends of the Earth are now focussing on the Act Local campaign in the run-up to the 2024 local and European elections.

Conclusions

It is essential in the battle to save the environment that people be informed as to the actions of mankind and provided with a place to discuss the issues facing them. Averaging two events a month, with low-level social media activity in support, suggests that the *Cuppa for Climate* campaign had only modest success in reaching people. While there are changes to be made to improve the social media reach, there are still grounds to feel that the campaign could be successful by being optimised with the correct use of social media, as these channels are the most effective space for both informing people and providing them with a place where they can discuss the issues. By combining this with the voluntary hosting of events tied to clearer activities, the message can be spread even wider, and it brings it into the mainstream which allows people to put pressure on governments to take more action. The plan to join this campaign to another makes sense for its future. This a simple fix but one based on evaluation, awareness and willingness to change. A better version of a *Cuppa for Climate* may emerge that will do justice to the efforts of its creators who remain passionate about their goals of putting conversations about the climate crisis firmly into everyday settings.

Explorations

1. How does this case study show that evaluation is a constant part of the communications process, and not only once a campaign has concluded?

2. What would you do to create a dialogue around climate change so that a tactic like coffee mornings could be more effective?

3. How might Burke's dramatism theory help create a compelling story for a *Cuppa for Climate*?

4. Examine the effectiveness of the use of social media channels in reaching target audiences.

5. What information would you put in a toolkit for a *Cuppa for Climate* coffee morning?

XIV. SDG 15 – Life On Land

Leave No Trace Ireland's *Love This Place* Campaign

Jade Marron

Abstract

Leave No Trace Ireland's annual campaign *Love This Place* addresses SDG 15 – Life on Land. This goal aims to protect, restore and promote sustainable use of terrestrial ecosystems, sustainably manage forests, combat desertification, and halt and reverse land degradation and halt biodiversity loss. The campaign began in 2020, when a spike in litter and environmental issues followed a sharp increase in the time people were spending outdoors. This was likely to combat the feeling of isolation that came with staying indoors to slow the spread of Covid-19. The campaign educates and raises awareness about enjoying the outdoors responsibility in order to protect wildlife, land, livestock, scenic locations and cultural heritage sites. The main messages of the campaign call on people to take their rubbish home with them, keep their dogs on a lead to avoid disturbing livestock, pick up their dog waste, stick to paths and trails so as not to disturb wildlife and vegetation, and avoid using campfires and disposable barbeques in undesignated areas, or if using them to ensure they are disposed of properly to mitigate the risk of fire devastation. The campaign has run annually since 2020 and has been successful in increasing reach and engagement each year. New tactics and activities were added each year to further the impact of the campaign. Leave No Trace Ireland also hope to begin multi-annual research in the years to come, to investigate whether its campaign has a direct correlation to public behaviour change.

Introduction

Leave No Trace Ireland is an outdoor ethics programme that works to provide research, education and initiatives to ensure people know how to protect and enjoy the Irish outdoors responsibly and sustainably. The organisation was established following agreement that stakeholders needed to work together to create a nationwide outdoor code across the island of Ireland. The educational approach in inspiring positive behavioural change and the ability to customise the seven principles to different settings resonated with stakeholders. Comhairle na Tuaithe, a non-statutory body established by the Irish government and comprising representatives of farming organisations, recreational users of the countryside, and State bodies with an interest in the countryside, agreed that Leave No Trace Ireland represented the best code of outdoor ethics for Ireland as it addressed a variety of needs relating to outdoor recreation. Launched in September 2008, Leave No Trace Ireland gained charitable status in 2013.

The organisation addresses a range of the UN SDGs, the most prominent being SDG 15 – Life on Land, which focuses on the protection, restoration and promotion of sustainable use of terrestrial ecosystems; sustainably managing forests; combatting deforestation; halting and reversing land degradation; and halting biodiversity loss. Leave No Trace Ireland contributes to this goal by inspiring ethical outdoor recreation through its seven core principles: plan ahead of time; be considerate of others; respect farm animals and wildfire; travel and camp on durable surfaces; leave what you find; dispose of waste properly; and minimise the effects of fire. Although its focus is SDG 15, the organisation and its campaign indirectly touch on SDG 3 – Good Health & Well-being, SDG 4 – Education, SDG 11 – Sustainable Cities & Communities, SDG 12 – Responsible Consumption & Production, SDG 13 – Climate Action, SDG 14 – Life Below Water, and SDG 17 – Partnerships for the Goals.

The goal of the *Love This Place* campaign is to educate and spread awareness on how to behave responsibly in the outdoors to protect the surrounding, flora, fauna and cultural sites. The organisation also wanted to make *Love This Place* and Leave No Trace Ireland a part of the people of Ireland's vocabulary.

Background

Throughout the Covid-19 lockdowns that began in 2020, Irish people spent around 55% more-time in the outdoors, turning to walking, hiking, running and spending time in nature. Mostly engaged in to escape from the isolation that came with staying indoors and away from others to slow the spread of the virus, these once relatively niche activities quickly became increasingly mainstream. People who had never climbed a mountain, camped, or swam in the ocean became regular visitors to the outdoors. While it was a health and well-being positive for new people to spend more time in the outdoors, there was a collective lack of awareness about how to behave responsibility to protect the surrounding nature. This was evident as scenic locations, including public parks, countryside and beaches became littering hotspots, especially when lockdown restrictions were eased. This was a threat to fragile ecosystems and the island's natural beauty.

Alongside the increase in people spending more time outdoors, staycations became extremely popular from 2021, when international travel was restricted. This also caused pressure points such as an increase of litter in the countryside and outdoor spaces, increase in dog fouling, dog worrying and attacks on farm livestock, and an increased risk of devastation caused by fire from campfires and barbecues that were not disposed of properly or allowed burn out of control.

Leave No Trace Ireland developed a campaign to raise awareness of the negative impacts of some segments of the public's lack of consideration for the natural environment around them, quickly launching the *Love This Place* campaign in 2020. Leave No Trace Ireland build a coalition of like-minded organisations including Sport Ireland, Fáilte Ireland, the National Parks & Wildlife Service, the Office of Public Works, Dublin City Council, the Department of Rural & Community Development, Waterways Ireland and Coillte. The campaign asked the public to exercise responsibility when spending time outdoors, with simple messaging of small actions with big positive outcomes. These included combatting littering by suggesting visitors to scenic places plan ahead and bring a bin bag to take rubbish home; being a responsible dog owner by picking up dog fouling, keeping pets on a lead to show consideration for others; being mindful of livestock and wildlife; and avoiding lighting campfires or using disposable barbeques unless they were on a designated site, and had both the permission of the landowner and the skills for setting and using campfires. The effective message that, when everyone plays their part, the public can collectively enjoy the outdoors while protecting the environment and preserving it for future generations under-pinned the campaign.

A successful start was encouraging, and the campaign was relaunched in 2021. Since then, there has been a consistent messaging campaign every summer. Each year has aimed to further the educational and promotional ambitions of protecting the environment when enjoying the outdoors, by creating targeted campaigns, and adding new targeted messages and activities as it evolves.

Tactics & Activities

Love This Place began in 2020 as a campaign with a simple concept. It focused on raising awareness on the negative impact of littering on the environment, in response to the increase in litter along scenic locations where people were picnicking or exercising in between lockdowns and restrictions across the country. The campaign consisted of a small number of assets strategically planned radio, television, and social media, including Facebook, Instagram and Twitter / X. This targeted audiences including those who were frequent and infrequent visitors to the outdoors and, especially those were new to spending increased time in the outdoors.

In summer 2021, the campaign was relaunched for eight weeks, maintaining its anti-littering message, and adding the additional focus of the correct disposal of campfires, single use barbeques and dog fouling that had become increasing issues as the number of staycations increased. With messages in both English and Irish, 28 graphics were used in the campaign, which also used radio advertising and social media to augment its messaging.

In 2022, the campaign continued messaging about the impacts of littering, irresponsible dog ownership and misuse of fires. However, it also added new messaging, asking those who enjoyed natural amenities to be considerate of others and to protect the surroundings so that other people could enjoy the outdoors. During this phase of the campaign, Leave No Trace Ireland commissioned a research survey, conducted by the polling company Behaviour & Attitudes. In terms of participation, the research found that in the summer of 2022, 75% of Irish people were walking or hiking weekly, and 25% were walking and hiking daily. In addition, another 25% were socialising in outdoor public places at least once a week, while 30% were participating in outdoor activities daily, and 81% were participating in outdoor activities weekly. The results of the survey revealed that there was growing awareness and understanding about the issues and messages Leave No Trace Ireland had communicated. However, while there was a growing desire to be more responsible, many, especially in the 18 to 34-year-old cohort, responded that they did not fully understand the behavioural changes needed to play a significant part in protecting the natural environment. This suggested to Leave No Trace Ireland that strong consistent messaging remained necessary.

The data enabled Leave No Trace Ireland to further identify behaviours specific to various groups of amenity users in its 2023 progression of the campaign, coupled with a change in tone. In 2023, the campaign continued to spread awareness on keeping Ireland litter-free, protecting wildlife, encouraging people to stick to paths to protect the land and the coasts, being responsible with dogs, and embracing cultural heritage. Building a broader coalition of support, the campaign was supported for the first time by many local authorities, including the county councils of Clare, Fingal, Galway, Kilkenny, Mayo, Wicklow and

Dun Laoghaire-Rathdown. Significantly, recognising that people seemed to have been constantly overwhelmed with negative news over the previous years, the organisation decided to change its messaging from a focus on the negative impacts of irresponsibility to a positive approach emphasising how people can play their part.

It was decided that the change would target the 18 to 34-year-old demographic, which had indicated the greatest levels of uncertainty about appropriate environmental behaviour. To reach this cohort, Leave No Trace Ireland brought Rozanna Purcell onboard as ambassador to the campaign. Purcell is an Irish presenter, broadcaster, content creator and founder of 'The Hike Life' page on social media. The Hike Life has over 170,000 followers and provides daily inspiration and information on hiking in Ireland. Purcell was chosen as ambassador as her following is in a similar demographic to those Leave No Trace Ireland was targeting in its 2023 campaign. She spends a lot of time outdoors with her hiking community and connects Leave No Trace Ireland's mission to enjoy the outdoors responsibility.

Engaging a well-known social media personality enhanced Leave No Trace's digital reach, as Purcell took part in various outdoor campaign activities, including several hikes, with Leave No Trace. During these events, she reiterated the organisation's messaging by encouraging her followers to attend and learn about responsible enjoyment of the outdoors, appreciation of the flora, fauna and cultural heritage. Among the most notable events she took part in was a Hike Life dog-friendly event, where people were encouraged to bring their pet and learn about responsible dog ownership in the outdoors. A clean-up hike brought participants together to pick litter as they hiked around Glendalough, an area of outstanding scenic beauty with cultural heritage extending over 1,500 years.

She also took part in promoting *Love This Place Day*, a new campaign initiative that took place on 28 July to coincide with *World Nature Conservation Day*. Purcell created content that she shared to her platforms encouraging engagement from the public. This day encouraged people to be part of the movement, to promise to *#LoveThisPlace* and to *#LeaveNoTrace* at the chosen hashtags. The messaging built on the consistency of previous years, but with a more positive tone, and reminded people of the simple actions they could take to keep Ireland litter-free, protect wildlife, stick to paths and be responsible with dogs and fires. The event called on people to take part in their own clean-up hikes and walks, or to share the *#LeaveNoPlacePledge* on their social media. An Instagram sticker was created for the public to tag Leave No Trace Ireland content in their Instagram stories. Alongside Instagram stories, Leave No Trace Ireland observed a significant increase in user generated content in TikTok and LinkedIn.

Results & Outcomes

Since 2020, the campaign has grown significantly. Leave No Trace Ireland measures the success of the campaign by how many people their messaging reaches, and the level of engagement from its publics. The daily listeners to radio messaging are calculated and digital analytics are used to determine the level of engagement online. In 2020, the once small campaign reached 2.9 million people through social media, radio and television, and social media engagement increased by 117% in comparison to 2019. These successful results provided an encouraging base for the campaign to re-emerge the following summer, when it reached over 4 million people, a significant increase from the year prior. Three million people heard the campaign on radio and over 4 million impressions were recorded across Leave No Trace Ireland's social media. Even at this early stage of the campaign, its impact was being noticed by communications and campaigning experts, and the organisation won the 2021 Charity Impact Award for medium-sized organisations in recognition of its work on the campaign.

In 2022, the campaign gained 4.9 million impressions online. There was a 1,253% increase in reach on its LinkedIn page and, despite a budget restriction on radio promotion, 3.1 million people heard the message on air approximately nine times each. That year, continuing the recognition of the campaign's effectiveness in generating environmental awareness, and sharing its methods and insights with like-minded organisations, Leave No Trace Ireland presented a seminar on the campaign, *Inspiring Ethical Outdoor Recreation*, at the Sustainable Outdoor Recreation conference in Snowdonia, Wales. This allowed its work to be shared at an international level and brought the Leave No Trace brand and ethos into the European sector.

The results of the 2023 cycle of the campaign were unavailable at the time of writing. However, initial expectations were for continuation of the success of the messaging and enhanced targeting of key publics, especially due to the engagement of Rozanna Purcell and greater emphasis on social media messaging. Anecdotally, the organisation observed that large numbers of its target publics created high-quality content tagging the organisation that was inspired by the campaign and its clear messaging.

Critical Analysis

The *Love this Place* campaign and its layered messaging each year has evidently been successful in spreading awareness about responsibility in the outdoors, as seen in the rising numbers of reach and engagement each year, particularly online and on radio. However, there is no available research in how successful the campaign has been in initiating public behaviour change. This is always difficult to measure accurately, and comes at a cost that can be prohibitive for small to medium-sized organisations. Leave No Trace Ireland plans to explore the campaign's impact with multi-annual research to see whether there is a direct correlation between its activities and a change in social behaviour.

Community participation is enhanced by the degree of connectedness publics feel to the discourse around an issue. The greater the knowledge publics have and the more positive their perception of a campaign, the greater their engagement. The *Love This Place* campaign increased the number of images used each year, including content of people engaging in their hikes and litter picking, and the archived public record of this campaign on Leave No Trace Ireland's social media channels suggests that the campaign was successful in informing publics and encouraging positive participatory behaviour. The images and videos there of people taking action on environmental issues also can increase perceived descriptive norms and group efficacy. This, in turn, creates has the possibility of increasing public intention on participating and taking action on behalf of the campaign.

Although the impact of celebrity influencers can be over-stated, there is anecdotal evidence and a reasonable belief that, when combined as education and communications, celebrity endorsements can promote sustained behavioural change. Initial large impacts sustained over a number of weeks result in only a small decline in the behavioural effect. This may be a good reason to continue with celebrity / influencer partnerships, especially due to the success of the collaboration with Rozanna Purcell. It may be useful in future campaigns to target multiple target groups, with particular assets designed to attract the attention to a range of demographics. This way it may achieve a larger more engaged audience.

Conclusion

The *Love This Place* campaign communicated by Leave No Trace Ireland and partners addresses SDG 15, by aiming to educate and raise awareness on issues that began to arise particularly after Covid-19 began to spread in 2020. These issues include spike in littering, dog fouling, livestock dog attacks, and incorrect or unauthorised use of campfires and disposable barbeques. Each year, campaign assets and layered messaging increased reach and engagement. The change to more positive messaging, the addressing of a particular target group, the collaboration with Rozanna Purcell and the national *Love This Place Day*, were particularly successful activities, as seen in the quality of user generated feedback inspired by the campaign. The campaign is expected to appear once again in the summer of 2024, continuing with positive messaging, and eventually Leave No Trace Ireland hopes to begin a multi-annual research analysis into the correlation between the campaigns and public behaviour change.

Explorations

1. The campaign made limited use of influencers, using only one well. What are the arguments for and against using influencers as a communications channel?

2. Given the ongoing nature of the campaign with new elements each year, what communications strategies could be used so that each year the campaign stays fresh and relevant?

3. Discuss how the campaign broke its audiences into distinct groups? Read Cliodhna Pierce's chapter for different theories of publics.

4. What are the factors to consider in 'coalition-building' for a campaign?

5. Do you agree with how the success of the campaign was measured? What other metrics might have been used?

XV. SDG 16 – Peace, Justice & Strong Institutions
Department of Justice / UN Migration Office in Ireland *Anyone* Campaign

Sarah-Kate Spratt

Abstract

This case study examines the *Anyone* campaign, a collaborative effort between the Department of Justice (DoJ) and the UN Migration Office in Ireland, addressing human trafficking in Ireland. Human trafficking, a global issue affecting over 50 million people, aligns with SDG 16, which emphasises peace, justice, and strong institutions. The *Anyone* campaign targets SDG 16 by aligning with specific targets, including ending abuse against children, curbing illicit financial flows, providing legal identity, and strengthening national institutions. The campaign, launched in 2021, aims to educate the public about human trafficking through various tactics. It includes releasing an impactful short film, *Anyone: Deceived*, and a dedicated website (www.anyonetrafficked.com) featuring informational videos, case studies, and resources. Social media platforms, especially Instagram, play a significant role in spreading awareness with the hashtag *#anyonetrafficked*.

Introduction

While speaking in a pre-recorded message for the premiere of *Anyone: Deceived*, a short film produced alongside the *Anyone* campaign, actor Tom Vaughan-Lawlor described human trafficking as "the recruitment of people through force or deception, then exploited for money of profit". Three elements, according to international law, are present in human trafficking: the act, the means, and the purpose.

The act refers to how the individual is brought into trafficking through recruitment, transportation or transferring, harbouring, or receipt of persons. The means refers to an individual who is trafficked and kept in the situation of being trafficked. It is usually carried out through the threatening of both the individual and their family, abduction, intimidation or harassment, or payment and benefits to the person in control of the victim. The victims are typically both mentally and physically harmed, while being isolated from both the outside world and potential help, reiterating their entrapment. The purpose is the reason trafficking has taken place; this usually involves financial persuasion for the trafficker. Human trafficking affects over 50 million people worldwide and generates approximately $150 billion *per annum* through sexual exploitation, forced labour, criminal activity, false marital situations, or the sales of removed organs.

SDG 16 is one of the 17 goals established by the United Nations in its 2030 *Agenda for Sustainable Development*. It aims at promoting peaceful and inclusive societies, providing access to justice for all, and building effective, accountable, and inclusive institutions at all levels. In the context of human trafficking, SDG 16 is particularly relevant due to its focus on issues related to peace, justice, and strong institutions. The targets that the *Anyone* campaign aligns with are as follows:

- **Target 16.2 - End Abuse, Exploitation, Trafficking & Violence Against Children:** The specific target is to end abuse, exploitation, trafficking, and violence against children. Human trafficking often involves the exploitation of vulnerable individuals, including children. Target 16.2 emphasises the need to address the root causes and consequences of trafficking, advocating for measures that protect children from exploitation and abuse. The *Anyone Trafficked* campaign aims to spread awareness to all potential victims, with no age restraint, and educate the public on recognising a situation of trafficking and knowing how to help those in need.
- **Target 16.4 - Curbing Illicit Financial & Arms Flows:** Victims of trafficking may be forced into situations to do with organised crime, leading to illicit financial flows. Target 16.4 calls for substantially reducing illicit financial and arms flow, aiming to significantly dismantle the networks that facilitate trafficking and related criminal activities.
- **Target 16.9 - Provide Legal Identity for All:** Lack of legal identity and documentation can make individuals more vulnerable to trafficking, as it creates a situation where they may be more easily exploited without legal recourse. SDG 16.9 emphasises the importance of providing legal identity for all, contributing to efforts to prevent and combat trafficking by ensuring that individuals have the legal means to protect themselves.

- **Target 16A - Strengthen National Institutions to Prevent Violence & Combat Crime:** SDG 16 recognises the crucial role of strong, accountable institutions in promoting peace and combating crime. Target 16.A focuses on strengthening national institutions to prevent violence and combat crime, including human trafficking. This involves improving the capacity and efficiency of law enforcement agencies, improving legal frameworks, and encouraging cooperation at national and international levels. The *Anyone* campaign promotes national cooperation and awareness, linking back to this target.

The Background

Human trafficking has been – and continues to be – a prevalent problem in Irish society. From 2015 to 2021, approximately 370 individuals were identified as victims of human trafficking. Many government and non-government organisations (NGOs) tackle the problem every year in hopes of eliminating it; however, each year, there are still cases and stories from survivors being shared and listened to. In June 2023, it was revealed that Ireland remains at Tier 2 in the US State Department's 2023 *Trafficking in Persons Report*. This sparked the notation that Ireland is on a human trafficking 'watchlist', which has given the country a less than desirable reputation within the field of human trafficking. This report has reiterated the need for the expulsion of trafficking in persons within Ireland, starting with education of the public to understand the signs of exploitation throughout the country.

The *Anyone* campaign is a collaborative effort between the DoJ and the UNMOI as part of their Blue Blindfold initiative. The public awareness campaign places emphasis on the reality that anyone may become a victim of human trafficking, as well as educating all members of the public on the signs of human trafficking to aid in putting an end to the issue. In 2022, the International Office of Migration (IOM) Ireland released an educational short film, *Anyone: Deceived*, as part of the campaign. The film's launch was attended by various Irish supporting parties, including the DoJ, the European Commission, the Director of Public Prosecutions, the Irish Human Rights & Equality Commission, Victim Support at Court, Health Service Executive, An Garda Síochána and the Irish NGO Ruhama.

The launch event facilitated multiple speakers such as the Head of the European Commission Representation in Ireland – Barbara Nolan, Ruhama's Chief Executive Officer – Barbara Condon, survivors of trafficking, IOM Ireland's Chief of Mission – Lalini Veerassamy, and pre-recorded speeches from the Minister of Justice – Helen McEntee and actor Tom Vaughan-Lawlor. The campaign was recognised by Ireland's Minister for Justice, Helen McEntee, in the 2023 *National Action Plan to Prevent & Combat Human Trafficking*. The Minister recognised the importance of campaigns that seek to raise awareness of the reality and signs of human trafficking, as well as the support services available to victims, stating that Ireland needs to be more alert to the reality of trafficking. She pledged support to the campaign as a vital action plan element.

Tactics & Activities

The largest scale activity launched within the *Anyone* campaign was that of the short film, *Anyone: Deceived*. The film followed two surviving victims of trafficking – a man and a woman – and told their stories: how they were drawn into the situation; how they lived through it and what was expected of them; why they could not escape straight away; and how they eventually got out of exploitation. The film detailed the everyday deceptions used to traffic individuals across the world, demonstrating how easy it can be for traffickers to draw victims in. The movie was released on 18 October 2022, the EU's *Anti-Trafficking Day*. A launch event was also held, with many government and public bodies in attendance. Speeches were given to share data and expertise among the group, updating them on the current climate of human trafficking in Ireland. The film has since been uploaded to the campaign's website to allow public access and exposure to the cause.

The campaign launched its own website (www.anyonetrafficked.com) as a platform for the public to educate themselves. The website includes short informational videos, case studies from victims who have survived a situation of trafficking, frequently asked questions and common misconceptions about human trafficking, education on the signs of trafficking, support services, and links to external pages such as social media platforms, the Blue Blindfold's independent website and contact links for An Garda Síochána.

The *Anyone* campaign used social media platforms (Facebook, Instagram, and Twitter / X) to spread the campaign's core message. IOM Ireland created, shared, and continuously used the hashtag – *#anyonetrafficked* – under its posts to do with the public awareness campaign. This hashtag created its own bubble of support from the public regarding the issue and gave social recognition to the campaign. In addition, short, informational videos, reels, were shared under this hashtag on Instagram. The information paired with this hashtag was concise, yet truthful and impactful, making for a clear aim of these posts, educating social media users on the campaign and its message. The campaign also collaborated with Bread 41, a prominent café in Dublin city centre, as presented on IOM Ireland's Instagram page on 10 December 2021. The post featured staff from IOM Ireland, DoJ, and Bread 41 to signify a united front between the public and private sector and the vitality of such partnerships to the issue of anti-trafficking.

The campaign also hosted a large outreach, which was mentioned in a National Action Plan, with the pledged support of the Minister for Justice in Ireland. The campaign's mission was spoken about, in addition to its importance and relevance in today's culture of trafficking in Ireland. The campaign's launch was also given its own announcement in a press release to speak about the conditions that led to the creation of the campaign, the main purposes and goals, and general information about IOM Ireland and DoJ's stance on human trafficking.

Critical Analysis

The *Anyone* campaign is a public awareness campaign to educate the general public on the reality of human trafficking, how it can happen, and how to understand and recognise the signs of a victim being trafficked. The campaign has produced many informational elements since its start in 2021 up to December 2023. As the campaign is ongoing, the results are unavailable and cannot be included in this analysis. However, the activities and tactics of the campaign to date are numerous, and so are eligible for analysis.

The launch of the short film *Anyone: Deceived* appears to be intended for an active audience, meaning that it most likely did not reach a large audience outside of the demographic in Ireland that is actively aware of human trafficking. While the film itself accurately and effectively depicts the unsettling nature of the culture of trafficking in Ireland, and educates those not well-versed in the topic, the audience reach had the potential to be larger through a more skilled use of social media.

The campaign's website also appears to be intended for an active public as it is somewhat of a specialised channel. The website itself is a useful instrument in understanding the campaign, gathering expert information, and understanding the severity of the climate of the trafficking of persons in Ireland. However, it is not widely promoted outside of IOM Ireland, DoJ, and the Blue Blindfold, meaning that if an individual is not actively seeking information about trafficking in Ireland, there is a strong likelihood that they may never come across it.

IOM Ireland headed most of the social media promotion for this campaign. While the hashtag – *#anyone* – was created and used under campaign posts, there appears to be a lack of numbers of these posts. Mass media sources, such as social media, are extremely useful tools for educating the passive audience. Creating more posts under the hashtag may have made for a bigger audience across social media platforms, reaching a demographic not previously educated on human trafficking. While the posts on social media were informative and cohesive, they appeared to have gradually come to a stop. An ongoing campaign should continuously promote the message behind their cause to reach the passive audience. There could also be more social media collaborations to promote the campaign further. Irish social media platforms could be contacted to gain a higher audience reach of both the hashtag and the posts that are linked to it.

A recommendation for campaign activities includes those that cater to a younger demographic. Collaborating with third-level institutions could reach an audience that has not already been directly educated through events such as panels of survivors speaking about their experience, especially those of a younger age, to reiterate that anyone could be a victim. In addition, throughout third-level education institutions, informational posters could be displayed throughout the grounds to strengthen the message to this age demographic. Collaborations with more private sector organisations could also be considered, including the *Anyone: Deceived* short film in preview line-ups in cinemas throughout the country to gain more exposure for the campaign and its message.

Conclusion

Human trafficking is an ongoing issue in that is not sufficiently covered in Irish media. The *Anyone* campaign is an effort to tackle this. The importance of educating the Irish public on human trafficking remains apparent. The campaign launched in 2021 and continues to run, operating through the efforts of both specialised and mass media to reach as many members of the public as possible. The campaign used a variety of activities to promote its message, and though they proved to be effective, recommendations have been listed above to improve outreach and exposure to the more passive public.

While the campaign has garnered support from government bodies and received recognition in the *National Action Plan to Prevent & Combat Human Trafficking*, this study suggests improving social media engagement, expanding collaborations, and targeting a younger demographic for a more comprehensive impact. The *Anyone* campaign serves as a vital initiative to combat human trafficking, emphasising the ongoing need for public education and engagement in Ireland, and the analysis concludes that there could be a more comprehensive outreach of public information. Overall and to date, the campaign has been effective in the strategies employed to spread awareness to the public and has launched many efforts to do so, gaining exposure from government bodies, internet sources (such as the campaign's own website and that of Blue Blindfold), and media sources.

Explorations

1. How might the *Anyone* campaign have tailored its messaging and channel selection differently for each audience segment to maximise impact?

2. What social media strategies could the campaign implement to increase engagement, reach a wider audience, and sustain momentum beyond initial launch activities?

3. What other types of partnerships could be beneficial in amplifying the campaign's message and reaching diverse audiences in Ireland?

4. The case study recommends targeting younger demographics: what elements could be explicitly introduced to engage younger audiences on the issue of human trafficking?

5. How could the campaign measure and report on its contribution to the SDGs?

Contributors

Nimra Ahmed was a member of the 25th cohort of the M.A. in Public Relations programme at TU Dublin. Nimra's areas of interest in PR are consumer, corporate, fashion, food, and hospitality sectors. Nimra's research curiosity is in fashion, artificial intelligence, mis- and dis-information, and deepfakes. She graduated with a B.A. in Journalism from TU Dublin.

Isaac Antwi-Boasiako is a Ph.D. candidate and assistant lecturer in the School of Media at TU Dublin. His doctoral research focuses on PR and public diplomacy from the Global South perspective. As an academic and researcher, Isaac has published several articles in peer-reviewed journals and presented academic papers at various conferences and symposiums. His research interests include strategic communications, Global South public diplomacy, international relations and ethics.

Gabriela Doleckova was a member of the 25th cohort of the M.A. in Public Relations programme at TU Dublin. Her research interests include corporate social responsibility, marketing, and not-for-profit public relations. Currently, she is researching social marketing with a focus on the importance of framing in health campaigns. Gabriela aspires to work in the non-profit sector or in a business committed to social consciousness.

Dr. Kevin Hora MPRII is Head of Discipline of Journalism & Communications in the School of Media, TU Dublin, and a graduate of the first cohort of the M.A. in Public Relations. His research interests are in the history and contemporary practice of strategic communications, and he has published and presented at international conferences in these areas. A member of the Public Relations Institute of Ireland, he is also an adjudicator on the Public Relations Consultants Association's national award for excellence.

Seán Ivory was a member of the 25th cohort of the M.A. in Public Relations programme at TU Dublin. Prior to joining the programme, he graduated with a B.A. in Communications Studies from Dublin City University.

David Little was a member of the 25th cohort of the M.A. in Public Relations programme at TU Dublin. He is a graduate of the university's B.A. in Journalism. David took up a position with CW8, founded by M.A. in Public Relations alumnus Colm Woods, while he completed his dissertation studies.

Dylan Mahon was a member of the 25th cohort of the M.A. in Public Relations programme at TU Dublin. Dylan graduated with a B.A. in Media Production & Digital Arts from TU Dublin. His research interests include sustainability and communications. He is looking to pursue a career in PR, such as developing content that effectively communicates and engages with the public.

Jade Marron was a member of the 25th cohort of the M.A. in Public Relations programme at TU Dublin. She has an International B.A. in Marketing & Psychological Studies from Maynooth University. Jade took up a position in the Dublin office of Wilson Hartnell while she completed her dissertation studies. She has previously worked for The Publicity Loft.

Avice Meya was a member of the 25th cohort of the M.A. in Public Relations programme at TU Dublin. With interests in international relations and sports diplomacy, Avice is keen to pursue research in human trafficking, immigration, and strategic communications. A professional international athlete, Avice aspires to be an ambassador promoting global positive change. Currently working on a Ph.D. proposal, Avice took up a position with Sport Ireland while she completed her dissertation studies.

Martha O'Brien was a member of the 25th cohort of the M.A. in Public Relations programme at TU Dublin. She graduated with a degree in Marketing from the National College of Ireland.

Molly Reilly was a member of the 25th cohort of the M.A. in Public Relations programme at TU Dublin. A graduate of Dublin City University with a B.A. in Communication Studies, she did her research on SDG 5 – Gender Equality, a topic that is important to her. She has a special interest in consumer and corporate PR, and aspires to work in these fields.

Dr. Cliodhna Pierce followed her University of Salford B.A. in TV & Radio Production with an M.A. in Public Affairs & Political Communications in TU Dublin (DIT). Her thesis on issues related to Freedom of Information requests earned the Hume Brophy Award. She completed a Ph.D. on the historical consequence of surveillance on the societies of Northern Ireland and East Germany during the 1970s and 1980s. With a professional career encapsulating over 10 years of PR, marketing and events, she is programme chair for the M.A. in Public Relations and M.A. in Public Affairs & Communications at TU Dublin.

Sarah-Kate Spratt was a member of the 25th cohort of the M.A. in Public Relations programme at TU Dublin. She holds a degree in Linguistics & Spanish from University College Dublin. Sarah-Kate took up a position with Harris PR while she completed her dissertation studies.

Tessa Thornton was a member of the 25th cohort of the M.A. in Public Relations programme at TU Dublin. She has a B.A. degree in Politics & International Relations, and History from University College Dublin. Tessa took up a position with 150Bond in its Dublin office while she completed her dissertation studies.

Eve Wright was a member of the 25th cohort of the M.A. in Public Relations programme at TU Dublin. She has a B.A. degree in World Religions & Theology from Trinity College Dublin. Eve took up a position with Walsh PR while she completed her dissertation studies.

www.ingramcontent.com/pod-product-compliance
Lightning Source LLC
Chambersburg PA
CBHW061254220326
41599CB00028B/5644